A HANDBOOK OF
PARISH
FINANCE

PHYLLIS CARTER AND
MICHAEL PERRY

Third Edition

MOWBRAY

Mowbray
A Cassell imprint
Villiers House, 41/47 Strand, London WC2N 5JE, England

First published 1981 by A. R. Mowbray & Co. Ltd.
Reprinted with revisions 1984
Third edition first published 1992
Reprinted 1993

British Library Cataloguing in Publication Data
A catalogue record for this book is available from the British Library.

ISBN 0–264–67279–8

Typeset by Fakenham Photosetting Ltd, Fakenham, Norfolk
Printed and bound in Great Britain by
Biddles Ltd, Guildford and King's Lynn

Contents

Mowbray Parish Handbooks

Introduction

The minister or parish treasurer who knows it all (or who thinks he knows it all) will not pick up this book, so we have no more to say to him. We have, instead, been writing for the person who feels inadequately informed about the financial affairs of the parishes of the Church of England and how they are conducted. Several groups of people have been in our minds as the manuscript progressed – PCC treasurers, obviously; the clergy, whose queries on various aspects of parish finances have often come our way; but beyond them, the many ordinary PCC members for whom the financial aspects of the work of the Church are a mystery, and all those people who are just plain curious about the Church and its money. Throughout, we have always tried to view finance from a parish standpoint. The person for whom we have particularly tried to write has been *either* the PCC member who knows a little about the business of the Church Council and has been persuaded into the job of treasurer, but feels that he knows very little about how books are kept; *or* the member of the congregation who has a good knowledge of financial procedures and, because of this, has been shanghaied onto the PCC to serve as treasurer, even though he doesn't know the difference between a rural dean and a reredos. The former wants to know the elements of book-keeping as they relate to Church accounts, and the latter wants basic information about how the Church is organized, and what the financial relationships are between parish, parson, diocese, and Church Commissioners.

This book is the result of a partnership between a former secretary to a Diocesan Board of Finance and an archdeacon. We feel a sympathy with all the people whose queries about parish finance we have had to deal with over the years, and we hope our experience may have taught us what questions are most frequently asked (and some of the answers to them). Our readers may occasionally find this book terribly elementary. That is because every treasurer has his own set of blind spots, and what seems simple to one may be a piece of arcane mystique to another. So we do not apologize for sometimes stating the obvious. On the other hand, parts of what follows may strike you as more complicated than your parish will ever need to know. That is not surprising. Parishes come in very different shapes and sizes. This handbook is not designed to blind you with science, only to be a resource-book. So skip what does not concern you, and only return to those pages when you find that you need them.

Our title is *A Handbook of Parish Finance*. Our concern, therefore, has been primarily financial, and legal questions have only been dealt with as they affect financial matters. A more legal treatment of many of the topics we deal with will be found in some of the books listed in Appendix 9 (p. 117 below). We recommend particularly *A Handbook for Churchwardens and Parochial Church Councillors*, in the same series as this book.

We would like to thank the Central Board of Finance of the Church of England for allowing us to make use of material of which they control the copyright – the text of Appendix 6.

Without a great deal of information, help, and advice, we could never have contemplated putting this volume together. In particular we would like to thank the heads of the relevant Departments of the Church Commissioners, the staffs of the General Synod, the Central Board of Finance of the Church of England (including their City Office), and the Church of England Pensions Board, Mrs S. R. Stapleton and the staff of the Ecclesiastical Insurance Office, and the Royal School of Church Music. The patience and thoroughness with which they have answered our queries, examined drafts of chapters and sections, and suggested alterations and deletions, has been a quite invaluable help to us. Our thanks also go to Alan Chesters, William Hurworth, Stuart Kitching, Alan Nugent and Kenneth Wills for their contributions to what has proved to be much more of a joint effort than a duet by the named authors. But in spite of all this expert help and advice, we cannot believe that we have got it all right. There may need to be further printings of this handbook, if it is found to be of any use at all; so if any reader discovers errors or omissions, we shall be glad to hear from him and to make subsequent editions more accurate than this present one.

Since this handbook was first published, there have been many changes in ecclesiastical and civil law which have made it necessary for us to rewrite large sections. We hope it may, in its third edition, be serviceable for the 1990s. For instance, despite our efforts, we have not always found it possible to avoid the use of the masculine pronoun.

Durham
August 1991

Phyllis Carter
Michael Perry

1

The Parochial Treasurer

In the most straightforward of cases, a minister is the incumbent of a single parish with its parish church and its Parochial Church Council. There is one set of church accounts, and the treasurer looks after them.

In the next chapter, we shall come to the possible complications; for the present, let us stick to the simple case. There is a legal framework within which this organization is set, and we had better look at the rules to see how the PCC is appointed, what its functions are, and where its treasurer fits into the system.

Every parish must hold, not later than 30 April each year, its annual parochial church meeting. This requirement is laid down in Rule 5(1) of the Church Representation Rules (see p. 117), which also lay down what business is to be transacted at the meeting; it includes the presentation of the audited accounts of the PCC and a report on the financial affairs of the parish. We will have a great deal more to say about those in Chapter 7.

The annual meeting also must elect the parochial representatives of the laity to the PCC. For a much more detailed presentation of the constitution and work of the PCC, see *A Handbook for Churchwardens and Parochial Church Councillors* (details on p. 117); meanwhile, let us note what are the general functions of the PCC. Section 6 (as amended) of the Synodical Government Measure 1969 defines them as follows:

(1) It shall be the duty of the minister and the parochial church council to consult together on matters of general concern and importance to the parish.
(2) The functions of parochial church councils shall include:
   (a) co-operation with the minister in promoting in the parish the whole mission of the Church, pastoral, evangelistic, social and ecumenical;

(b) the consideration and discussion of matters concerning the Church of England or any other matters of religious or public interest, but not the declaration of the doctrine of the Church on any question;

(c) making known and putting into effect any provision made by the diocesan synod or the deanery synod, but without prejudice to the powers of the council on any particular matter;

(d) giving advice to the diocesan synod and the deanery synod on any matter referred to the council;

(e) raising such matters as the council consider appropriate with the diocesan synod or the deanery synod.

(3) In the exercise of its functions the parochial church council shall take into consideration any expression of opinion by any parochial church meeting.

It is obvious that the PCC has wide responsibilities, not all of which are financial in nature. They are, however, all part of the Church's mission, and they form the context within which the financial business of the Church needs to be seen.

Once the PCC has been elected, at the first meeting following the annual parochial church meeting, it must appoint its officers. The treasurer is one of them. His appointment (and many of them are female, but we will use the masculine term for convenience and to include both) is governed by Appendix II of the Church Representation Rules which provides, *inter alia*:

> 1(e) The council may appoint one or more of their number to act as treasurer solely or jointly. Failing such appointment, the office of treasurer shall be discharged jointly by such of the churchwardens as are members of the council, or, if there is only one such churchwarden, by the churchwarden solely. No remuneration shall be paid to any person in respect of his appointment as treasurer.

There is a distinct advantage in having a treasurer who is not also a churchwarden, though in some small parishes this may not always be possible. It is wise to involve as many lay people as possible in the work of the Church, so that the tasks of running the parish, keeping the church building and other property in good repair, and forwarding the whole mission of the Kingdom of God, can be widely shared. In this way the Church can gain different insights from lay people, who will be encouraged to use their God-given talents in his service.

The rules do not forbid the incumbent to be treasurer, but it should be regarded as a really desperate expedient to do so. Some parsons, of course, find delegation a difficult art; some are convinced that there is nobody in their congregation competent to do the job of treasurer; some members of PCCs are remarkably backward in coming forward when jobs are being handed out. None of these reasons ought willingly to be accepted as a justification for forcing the minister (or minister's spouse) to become treasurer. In the first place, this is not his function in the parish; secondly, it may help to avoid any possible criticism if the finances are handled by someone separate from the parson and his household; and thirdly, when the parson is away or ill, when he moves to another parish or retires or dies in office, the parish will find itself in great difficulties if there remains no one who understands its finances.

The Church Representation Rules provide for a standing committee of the PCC, which is to be appointed at the first meeting after the annual meeting. Besides the minister and churchwardens ex-officio, 'the council shall by resolution appoint at least two other members of the standing committee from among its own members and may remove any person so appointed'. The Rules go on to state that 'the standing committee shall have power to transact the business of the council between the meetings thereof subject to any directions given by the council'. It would be strange if the treasurer were not to be a member of this Standing Committee. It can form a group, or 'inner cabinet' of the parish, which discusses with the minister the parish strategy, at which ideas and plans are floated, and which makes recommendations to the PCC which frequently have financial implications.

Other committees may be appointed for specific purposes in connection with various kinds of church work in the parish; these may include persons who are not members of the PCC. The minister is a member of all committees ex-officio and if their recommendations are likely to involve finance, it is probably wise to ensure that the treasurer is also an invariable member. He will use his discretion (after a period of experience) to decide whether he needs to attend all meetings of such committees.

The treasurer must be chosen by the PCC from among its membership. It may happen that the person whom the PCC believes could best serve as treasurer is not a PCC member. In that case, there is no objection to his being made a co-opted member. Once the PCC has co-opted him and he has accepted co-optation, he is as much a PCC member as any other, and the Council can then elect him treasurer. Note, however, that co-opted members may not exceed one-fifth of the elected members of the council.

The treasurer should always try to be present at PCC meetings. Even if nothing explicitly financial is under discussion, he ought to know (and have a say in) the plans of the parish as a whole. If he has to be absent from any PCC meeting, the secretary should notify him as soon as possible of any discussion or decisions of a financial nature.

When the PCC and/or its standing committee plan the work and mission of the Church in the parish, the treasurer's responsibility is to advise on the financial implications of any proposals which are made. While that means that the treasurer needs realistically to assess the parish's resources before giving his advice, Christians should always take care to ensure that money is the servant and not the master. Sometimes there may not be enough money in the bank to carry out a particular course of action; but if it is the right course of action, if it is fully explained, and if it catches the imagination of the congregation, then (more often than not) the money will be forthcoming. That is why the treasurer needs to be more than simply the man who knows how to keep a cash book. He needs to understand the mission of the Church in the parish, and to have a 'feel' for what is right (and possible) at a particular juncture. He ought to be able to appreciate the Church's 'needs and resources', and to know that 'needs' and 'resources' are not only measured in monetary terms. The 'needs' of the Church include the need to proclaim the whole Gospel to the whole world (and the 'needs' of the world include the world's need for the Gospel, which it may not want but certainly needs). The 'resources' of the Church can be defined so as to include the abilities and depth of commitment of church members, and – supremely – defined in terms of the infinite resources of God, who calls men and women, and who enables men and women to respond to his call.

As the commitment of men and women to God grows and deepens, so they give themselves more fully (in money and in talents) to him, and so the resources of the Church expand. Leadership plays a vital role in all this, because, without vision, the Church becomes introverted and unable to see beyond the parish pump. And 'leadership' should be not simply the lone exhortations of the clergyman, but something which flows out of a team of minister(s) and people, working together and energized by God's Holy Spirit. Sadly, the work of some ministers with vision can be thwarted if their laity are unwilling to accept a proffered share in leadership. Equally sadly, the reverse can happen if the minister is unwilling to offer it. In both cases, there is often need to relinquish entrenched ideas or prejudices, and this calls for great sensitivity and mutual understanding, which do not come about automatically.

All of this shows what a crucial position is held by the PCC treasurer. Who is sufficient for all these things? When faced with an invitation to become treasurer, a person may well feel daunted. That is no bad thing. It shows that the position is being taken seriously. This book cannot help much in the area of Christian commitment, or of sympathetic engagement within team planning in a parish. Where we hope it *may* be of use is in the more practical, 'nuts-and-bolts', business of explaining to the PCC treasurer and other members of the PCC where the Church's money comes from, where it goes to, and what the treasurer has to do with it in between. Off we go, then!

2

The Parish and its Staff

Parish and benefice

If the treasurer gets clear in his own mind the distinction between *parish* and *benefice*, he will be saved a great deal of confusion.

A *parish* is a geographical area. The bishop commits the cure (or care) of souls of the parishioners to a minister who thereby becomes the incumbent of the parish. (Incumbents are called either rectors or vicars, but the distinction nowadays has no practical effect.) Each parish has churchwardens and a parochial church council. Most parishes contain a parish church; some also have daughter churches or other places where there is Anglican worship, and occasionally there can be a parish with two or more parish churches.

A *benefice* is the office of rector or vicar and the financial, property-owning, and legal benefits which belong to that office. Certain rights and endowments belong to the benefice and are enjoyed by the incumbent for the time being, who holds these (as it were) in trust and is not allowed to sell or otherwise dispose of them while incumbent of the benefice except under strict conditions. Usually the parsonage house is benefice property, as is the land surrounding it. Until 1978 glebe also used to belong to the benefice, but it is now (under the Endowments and Glebe Measure 1976) owned and administered by the diocese, under controls exercised by the Church Commissioners in London.

The term *benefice property* is used to denote property belonging to the benefice and not under the control of the parochial church council. *Parish property* is property in the possession of the PCC or of the incumbent and churchwardens. In neither benefice nor parish property, however, does the 'owner' necessarily have a free hand as to what is done with the property. Benefice property cannot be sold or leased, demolished or added to, without certain consents (notably of the diocese and the Church Commissioners), and parish property

is often held on trusts (frequently with the Diocesan Board of
Finance as custodian trustee). Some church halls were established
under educational trusts and therefore involve the Diocesan Board
of Education and/or the Department of Education and Science (see
p. 37 below). And although the incumbent's house is (with a few
exceptions) benefice property, dioceses will look to parishes for contributions either through the diocesan quota or separately to supplement the grants which are available from the Commissioners for
repairs, rates and improvements, and even for new houses. As for
the church building and churchyard, the PCC knows how much of
its money goes towards their maintenance and upkeep; but legally,
the freehold ownership vests in the incumbent for the time being,
whilst possession of church and churchyard is vested in the incumbent and churchwardens jointly. The churchwardens are the legal
owners of movable furniture and ornaments of the church, but the
clergy are entitled to the use of any objects which they require in the
course of their ministrations. The removal, alteration or addition of
objects in the church and churchyard is controlled by the Faculty
Jurisdiction Measure 1964 as amended by the Care of Churches and
Ecclesiastical Jurisdiction Measure.

Church property is a large and complicated subject and the foregoing paragraph is a simplified description to which there are exceptions in occasional cases. The parish treasurer should realize that,
whoever is regarded as owning the church and churchyard, 'the
care, maintenance, preservation and insurance of the fabric of the
church, and of the goods and ornaments thereof, and the repair of
the churchyard fence and other structures are, under the modern
law, the responsibility of the parochial church council'.[1]

Unions, teams and groups

The simple pattern is for one minister to be given his benefice and to
look after a single parish with its parish church. It is possible,
however (and increasingly frequent), for there to be pluralities,
unions of benefices, unions of parishes, team ministries and group
ministries. What do these involve?

If two benefices are held in plurality, one minister is the incumbent of two distinct benefices. The parishes remain completely
separate; each parish has its own parish church, churchwardens,
PCC, treasurer, and PCC accounts.

When two (or more) benefices are united but the parishes are not,
the result is (for most day-to-day purposes) the same as a plurality.

[1] *A Handbook for Churchwardens and Parochial Church Councillors* by K. M. Macmorran, E.
Garth Moore and Timothy Briden (Mowbray, 1989 edition), p. 71.

Each parish retains its own individuality, though the parishes share a minister – and have to agree among themselves as to the division of their financial responsibility for housing and expenses of office.

A union of benefices *and* parishes results in the formation of a single unit out of what were separate benefices and parishes, so that the new unit is a single parish with a single PCC. The Scheme which creates the new parish may designate more than one parish church, and it may also state which is to be the parsonage house of the benefice. If there are two or more centres of worship it is possible, under Rule 16 of the Church Representation Rules, for the annual meeting to make a scheme for the election of district church councils. They may have their own churchwardens, treasurers and accounts, but there is only one PCC. The accounts for each district must be presented to the annual meeting.

In some parishes, daughter churches have been built to serve particular areas within the parish. The annual meeting can delegate some of the PCC's functions to district church councils, and the daughter churches may have their own wardens, treasurers and accounts; but, again, overall control is vested in the PCC, which retains ultimate authority over the daughter church's finances. All accounts are parish accounts, subject to audit, and scrutinized at the annual meeting (of which more in Chapter 7 below).

Team or group ministries are set up under the provisions of the Pastoral Measure 1983. A team ministry is a single benefice, served by a team rector and team vicars, though there may be more than one PCC. Group ministries, as the name implies, are ministries covering two or more benefices and parishes with different incumbents, each of which has its own PCC and financial organization. For further details, consult *A Handbook for Churchwardens and Parochial Church Councillors* (1989 edition), pp. 24–5 (see p. 117 below).

In a group, there may be a group council for the group as a whole, to facilitate co-ordinated work within the area. The PCCs may decide to make grants to enable a group council to open its own bank account, in which case the group council will need to appoint its own treasurer. This may be of assistance if, for instance, there is a group magazine in place of separate parish magazines, and the printer's bills are paid and the advertisers' charges received by the group, which then sells bulk orders to the separate parishes. On the whole, however, it would probably be more simple to pass group expenses through PCC accounts, and for financial adjustments to be made by arrangements between the treasurers on PCC authorization. If there is a separate group account and treasurer, that account should be audited annually like the other parish accounts, and the audited statement presented at the annual meeting of each parish in the group.

Shared churches and local ecumenical projects

The Sharing of Church Buildings Act 1969 enables two or more churches of different denominations to make 'sharing agreements' for sharing 'church buildings'. The types of building which may be 'shared' and the churches which may be a party to any such 'sharing agreement' are set out in the Act. This is a complex piece of legislation, which (although many churches are already shared) does not affect the majority of PCCs in the country. Before any such agreement is signed, approval must be obtained from the Diocesan Board of Finance and the Diocesan Pastoral Committee, and the financial implications (e.g. heating, lighting, repair etc.) should be discussed thoroughly by the denominations concerned, so that each is quite clear as to the extent of its responsibilities.

The agreement will define the extent to which a church is to be available for worship in accordance with the forms of service of the sharing churches, also for joint services on such occasion as may be approved by the churches concerned; and the proportions in which the participating denominations share financial responsibility.

In most local ecumenical projects there will be sponsoring bodies which are independent of the PCC and the local committees of other denominations, sometimes holding and administering funds provided by the diocese and its equivalent in the other churches of the project.

If there are joint services the treasurer and members of the local council should bear in mind that there may be accountability not only to the Church of England but also to, say, the Methodist or the United Reformed Church central bodies.

In such areas there are no hard and fast rules about shared finance, so there needs to be extra 'sensitivity' and understanding of administration on a wider basis than the Church of England.

The incumbent

When a benefice is vacant, the patron presents to the bishop a suitable minister, who then is instituted to the benefice. (If the bishop is himself patron, 'institution' is termed 'collation'.) Once the minister has been instituted by the bishop and inducted into the temporalities of the benefice by the archdeacon or his representative, he holds the freehold of the benefice and can only be removed, after due legal process, for a breakdown in pastoral relationships or some misdemeanour, unless he resigns voluntarily or reaches the age of 70 years. (Incumbents who were in their present office before the Ecclesiastical Officers (Age Limit) Measure 1975 took effect on 1 January 1976 are not bound to retire when they reach the age of 70.)

Team ministers

A team ministry is governed by a Scheme prepared by the Church Commissioners after extensive local consultation, and confirmed by Her Majesty in Council, notice of which is published in the *London Gazette*. The incumbent of a team ministry is the team rector, and the Scheme will give details of which person, office-holder, or body is to be the patron of the benefice, and will state whether the appointment of rector is to be freehold (i.e. until the rector attains retirement age) or leasehold (i.e. for a specified number of years, in which case the appointment is generally renewable). The Scheme will state how many team vicars there are to be within the area of the benefice. Team vicars, who are also of incumbent status, are usually appointed by the bishop and team rector jointly, but if a team rector is to be presented by a patronage board or by a diocesan board of patronage, the team vicars can also be chosen by the same body. They hold their office leasehold for a specified number of years. They are not instituted, but hold the bishop's licence. The licence may define the team vicar's duties or the area of his responsibility within the team, or this may be left for negotiation between the team rector and team vicar. There is power for the bishop to issue an 'Instrument under his hand' to provide for district church councils under the authority of the PCC to administer any other places of worship in the team, and any other administrative matters, or in a multi-parish team to establish a team council; the DCCs may have their own treasurers and accounts, but the accounts are subject to audit and presentation at the annual parochial church meeting. It is not, however, legally necessary for there to be DCCs, and if the parish so wishes it can decide to have one PCC account and one treasurer, irrespective of the number of places of worship in the 'team' parish.

Besides officially-constituted team ministries, there are many unofficial teams of parishes whose incumbents and staffs meet regularly for prayer, discussion, and fellowship. Such associations are entirely voluntary, but are much to be encouraged as helping to prevent ministers from becoming isolated within their own parishes, unaware of the Church beyond the parish boundaries, and unhelped by their colleagues in the ministry.

Group ministries

A group ministry is a much looser organization than a team, and in it the parishes concerned remain distinct. Once, however, a group ministry has been set up by Order in Council of Her Majesty, it is as legally binding as the creation of a team. Each incumbent in a group has authority to perform, within any benefice of the group, all such offices and services as the incumbent of that benefice may himself perform. The incumbents are under a duty to assist each other, so as to make the best possible provision for the cure of souls throughout the whole area of the group. When any incumbency within the group falls vacant, the patron must obtain the bishop's approval of the person presented, and the bishop is required to consult with all the other incumbents in the group before reaching his decision. The parishes and their finances remain distinct.

Ministers-in-charge

A 'conventional district' may be created out of parts of one or more parishes, with the consent of the incumbent(s) concerned, and will have its own minister-in-charge appointed by the bishop. A conventional district is generally formed within a new housing area in anticipation of its eventually becoming a parish in its own right. Once it has been formed, it has its own church building, churchwardens and church council, which function for all practical purposes as though the district were a full parish. Parishioners, however, retain rights within the original parish church if they wish to exercise them. Ministers-in-charge have no freehold, but are licensed by the bishop. The licence does not specify any term of years but may be revoked at the bishop's discretion.

Sometimes, for reasons approved by the Diocesan Pastoral Committee (generally concerned with long-term plans for pastoral reorganization), the patronage to any benefice may temporarily be suspended. Then, instead of the patron appointing an incumbent with freehold, the bishop appoints a minister-in-charge whom he licenses and whom he is free to remove at his discretion. Such ministers-in-charge are for most purposes indistinguishable from incumbents.

Assistant ministers

An assistant curate must be nominated to the bishop by the incumbent of the parish (or the minister-in-charge of the conventional district) in which he is to work. Subject to certain legal formalities, the bishop then licenses him.

Deacons, deaconesses, Church Army officers, members of religious communities, and lay workers (male and female), if they receive a stipend for working in a parish, are appointed by the incumbent but have to be licensed by the bishop.

Stipends

Nearly all clergy of incumbent status and assistant staff now receive a monthly payment and statement from the Church Commissioners.

How are stipends made up?

Most assistant staff receive almost the whole of their stipend from a fund held by the Church Commissioners called the Diocesan Stipends Fund. This is made up partly of money that the Church Commissioners have allocated to dioceses over the years, but also of money raised by Church people in the parishes (see below), and income from diocesan glebe.

Incumbents, however, tend to receive their income from a variety of sources. In 1975 the General Synod decided that certain of these should be 'taken into account' before a calculation was made as to the amount by which the stipend should be 'topped-up', or augmented from the Diocesan Stipends Funds to the level decided on by the diocese. The sources are:

(i) former endowments of the particular benefice (now called guaranteed annuities or personal grants and held by the Church Commissioners);

(ii) parochial giving direct for stipend purposes (which should now normally be channelled through the diocese and the Church Commissioners);

(iii) Easter Offerings;

(iv) fees (both parochial and non-parochial – e.g. crematorium fees);

(v) net income from chaplaincies and public and educational appointments; and

(vi) income from local trusts.

(The computation was not to include spare-time earnings, a spouse's earnings, private income, or income from the informal letting of parsonage rooms.)

So (to take an illustration that is now purely historic) if the annual income from all the above sources was £1,500 and the stipend the diocese had decided upon was £12,000, an augmentation grant of £10,500 would be paid from the Diocesan Stipends Fund.

Fees

Under the Ecclesiastical Fees Measure 1986, incumbents and ministers-in-charge receive payment for providing a baptism certificate (but not for performing the service), for calling banns, making searches in registers, allowing monuments to be erected in churchyards, and for surplice fees (weddings and funerals). Fees payable to a minister for officiating at a burial or cremation elsewhere are fixed by the local authority or burial board which administers the burial ground, cemetery, or crematorium. Fees laid down by the Orders under the 1986 Measure are payable to the incumbent by virtue of his office, and are not strictly receivable by team vicars, curates or lay workers, although in some cases local arrangements are made whereby the particular fee may be paid to the person actually officiating. Many incumbents now assign their fees to the diocese, others choose to retain them and stipend levels are adjusted accordingly. All these fees form part of the minister's official income. He must declare them to the diocese, Church Commissioners, and the Inland Revenue (see also p. 85 for fees payable to PCCs).

In the computation for augmentation purposes referred to opposite, fees are usually assessed for a year at a time, and the augmentation grant is therefore based on an estimate. This can mean that, in the short term, the incumbent's income is variable, depending on how many weddings and funerals he conducts in a particular month; but a diocese will ensure that he does, in the end, receive (at least) the full annual stipend that has been decided on.

How are the levels settled?

Each year, the Church Commissioners, acting as Central Stipends Authority (CSA), make recommendations after extensive consultation with diocesan representatives, about stipend levels to apply throughout the country. They recommend a national minimum stipend for incumbents and other clergy of incumbent status (such as team vicars and full-time ministers-in-charge), and a maximum average stipend, intended as a ceiling for dioceses, so as to minimize variations between different parts of the country, but the diocesan authorities have complete freedom to decide on particular stipend levels to be paid to individual incumbents. The CSA also publishes recommended national scales (related to years of service) for assistant staff.

Although the Commissioners make the actual stipend payments, they would not be able to do so without substantial help from Church people in the dioceses. Their investment income has to provide for the rising cost of pensions as well, so the cost of stipends is increasingly falling on parish quotas/shares. Each diocese has to decide how much money it needs to raise for the Diocesan Stipends Fund. The figure will depend on the levels it decides to aim at within the CSA's recommended stipend range for the year in question, the number of ministers on the payroll, and the amount made available by the Commissioners to the diocese. Each diocese then has to decide how it is to raise the amount it needs. Some dioceses do this by asking parishes to pay a quota/share based on their actual income, some by assessing an agreed 'potential income' and asking for a percentage of this. Some dioceses have a consolidated diocesan budget, others have two separate budgets – one administrative and the other a stipend or ministerial budget. In one or two dioceses, parishes are asked to make their contributions direct to the minister concerned, but in all other cases the moneys pass through the diocese and Church Commissioners so that the minister receives a single monthly payment from one source. The treasurer who wants to know local practice should ask the diocesan office.

National Insurance and tax

Whether or not a minister has a freehold office, *for the purposes of National Insurance* (and for those purposes *only*), ministers are classified as 'employed persons' and pay the National Insurance contribution appropriate to employed, not self-employed, persons. The same is true of assistant staff, although they are regarded as office-holders for purposes other than National Insurance. This means that the clergy and layworkers are eligible for maternity, sickness and industrial injuries benefits as well as for the same kind of index-linked pensions benefits as any other employed person. The Church Commissioners are designated as the 'employer' for this purpose (only) and so they pay the employer's NI contribution, as well as deducting the employee's contribution from the stipend. However, if a minister or lay worker makes a claim for industrial injuries benefit, the Commissioners will normally ask a diocesan representative to act on their behalf when filling in the employer's part of the claim form.

The Church Commissioners are responsible for the deduction of income tax according to the PAYE code, in accordance with Inland Revenue regulations.

Housing

In the rare cases where an incumbent's house does not belong to the benefice but is owned, for example, by the PCC or a Trust, the owners will be responsible by agreement with the incumbent for arranging who pays for what outgoings. (There may be an arrangement with the diocese whereby financial help is available from funds at the disposal of the Diocesan Board of Finance.) In the normal case, where the incumbent lives in a house which is benefice property, the Diocesan Parsonages Board (or Committee) is legally responsible for the repair and insurance of the house. Informally, all dioceses also ensure that the incumbent is relieved of water rate , rent and loan repayments. The money to pay for repairs and other outgoings is provided partly by the Commissioners (about half) and partly by the dioceses, which usually have to raise most of the balance from parishes, either through the diocesan quota/share, through a special parsonage contribution, or by making parishes responsible for meeting particular outgoings, e.g. water rate.

Improvements are a matter for negotiation between diocese and parish (and may involve the Church Commissioners as well) and the relative financial contributions are a matter for mutual agreement in the light of individual circumstances. Interior decorations are the responsibility of incumbents, and arrangements for assisting them differ from diocese to diocese. Sometimes designated funds are available to assist with this, but each diocese has its own way of organizing this. The insurance of the contents of the parsonage as distinct from the insurance of the fabric of the house itself is entirely a matter for the incumbent (though the PCC may wish to help pay the premium – see p. 55 below).

By arrangement with the Inland Revenue, the Church Commissioners allow the cost of heating, lighting and cleaning of the parsonage and the upkeep of the garden as a non-taxable part of the stipend. 'Lighting' includes the cost of replacing electric light bulbs; 'cleaning' includes the wages of a cleaner (or of the incumbent's spouse or members of the family if an agreed and appropriate wage is paid for this service), but not the wages of anyone who does cooking or laundry or other similar services; and 'garden upkeep' includes gardener's wages and the cost of motor mower repair and upkeep and petrol, but not the purchase of new equipment, tools, or mower, or the cost of plants, seeds, shrubs, etc. The exact amount of such non-taxable reimbursement is agreed between the incumbent and the Commissioners, who ask the secretary of the Diocesan Board of Finance and the bishop (or someone whom he designates for this purpose) to examine and certify all claims. If the PCC makes any financial contribution to heating, lighting, cleaning and garden upkeep, this contribution, which is itself taxable, must be set against the tax-free proportion of the minister's stipend. These arrangements apply to full-time incumbents and assistant clergy, providing their houses are owned either by the benefice or by a charity. Certain stipendiary lay workers also qualify, if their status is agreed with the Inland Revenue. If the accommodation is rented, it is necessary to ensure that the lease or rent book is in the name of the PCC or some ecclesiastical body (e.g. the DBF). The occupant can then receive that proportion of his stipend which he spends on heat, light, cleaning and garden upkeep, free of income tax. If the lease is in his own name, this is not possible.

The Central Stipends Authority requires that all assistant staff should be provided with accommodation free of rent, water rate , insurance, and repair charges (exterior painting to count as repairs). An appropriate allowance should be paid in lieu if a house or flat is not provided. Guidelines on this are available from the CSA. If a person is living in 'digs' and pays a weekly amount which includes food and other services, then agreement must be reached as to the 'accommodation' part of the weekly payment. The diocesan office will tell you which of these charges is in your diocese customarily paid by the diocese and which by the PCC.

Working expenses

The clergy and lay workers (whether working full-time or part-time) ought not to be expected out of their own very limited stipends to help towards the cost of running the parish. It would be unheard-of for an office worker in government, industry or commerce to have to pay his firm's postage costs, business travel expenses, telephone bills etc. In the Church, the laity have for too long acquiesced in a situation where the parson pays many of these expenses and nobody thinks it odd. In too many parishes, there is still resistance on the part of some of the laity to making these payments – in full – a first charge on the budget of the PCC. Yet anything less than this is an inadequate goal to aim at.

The Central Stipends Authority (Church Commissioners) defines working expenses as including the following:

> Postage; stationery; telephone; public transport; car running and depreciation; cost of secretarial assistance; hospitality; provision and depreciation of office equipment; maintenance of robes; provision of locum tenens.

On this definition, the Central Stipends Authority points out that in 1990, the average incumbent paid 15 per cent of the cost of the running expenses of the parish, and the PCC average contribution was only 85 per cent. With expenses averaging £1,482 per parish, that meant the average incumbent paid £215 to enable himself to do the work of his parish. Assistant curates and lay workers incurred lower expenses and were on average repaid slightly more by the PCCs; but 100 per cent reimbursement is still a long way ahead. The minister who meets some of the expenses of running his parish may claim that cost as non-taxable when he makes his annual tax return, but that is not good enough. He ought to get the amount in full from his PCC. Some clergy like to make a gift of all or part of these expenses to their parishes. That is their own business, but it would be far better if they claimed their expenses in full, so that the PCC and the treasurer knew the real cost of administration in the parish; they could then repay that amount as a gift (under a deed of covenant if possible) to the PCC. That would also avoid embarrassment and difficulty when a new minister arrives and is unwilling or unable to continue the practice of his predecessor.

It follows that the treasurer should acquaint himself with the working expenses of all the parish staff. He should discuss the amounts with the incumbent, and it is particularly desirable that he should try (probably with the help of the churchwardens) to come to some measure of provisional agreement with the incumbent about the amount of expenses that should properly be reimbursed. The treasurer can then present the case to the PCC. Many incumbents find it embarrassing to make such requests direct to the PCC, and it is much more satisfactory if this can be done by a lay official. When the case has been put to the PCC, that body should realize that any failure fully to reimburse such expenses is in effect to reduce the stipend of the minister by that amount.

How are the relevant figures to be arrived at? Postages and stationery are easy to define, provided the minister keeps an account of his expenditure. For telephone and car expenses, it is not so simple. Some PCCs pay the whole cost of the telephone irrespective of personal use; others, after discussion, agree to pay the rental plus a fixed percentage of the cost of calls; others pay a percentage of the total bill (rental plus calls) to take account of personal use.

A car (which can be ruinously expensive, but is usually essential to the efficient working of a parish) presents other problems in assessing a fair division of cost. The PCC must decide (after taking the advice of the treasurer who will have talked this over with the incumbent) whether to pay a fixed sum, or a mileage allowance, or to pay tax and insurance together with a depreciation and/or mileage allowance. Agreement may not be easy to come by because different people have different ideas about how essential a car is, but it is important that the attempt should be made. The CSA recommends a mileage allowance, as fixed sums to cover standing costs are taxable. Whilst it is true that a particular visit or attendance at a particular meeting could have been made on foot, bicycle, or on public transport, it is equally true that the clergy have to be good stewards of their time, and the more time they spend walking to meetings or waiting at bus stops, the less time they have for the work of the parish.

Secretarial assistance may be paid for direct by the PCC as 'employer', or if the minister is 'employer', then expenses will require reimbursement. In appropriate cases, the spouse may be paid, but all should be satisfied that the person concerned is performing useful duties beyond the call of the family. Any such payment where clergy pass cash to the spouse should not be made as a means of reducing tax liability; the Inland Revenue could well disallow a claim if the PCC is not asked to make a contribution towards payment.

Office equipment depends upon the size of the parish, but where appropriate, typewriters/word processors, microcomputers and photocopiers may be essential. If a minister owns some or all of these items, an allowance for appropriate use, based on depreciation, and running costs will be required.

Provision, replacement and repair of robes should be considered by the PCC and the extent of provision may be governed by tradition. Hospitality is very difficult to quantify, but due consideration should be given to expenditure on even the most basic items such as tea and coffee if the number of cups poured each week is significant.

Where clergy are visiting a parish, their expenses should be met in full.

Other items worth considering are books and periodicals, if they are helpful for the parish or aid the minister pastorally or in teaching; furniture and furnishings in the 'official' parts of the house, especially the study; and support for in-service training, if not centrally funded.

How is this budgeted for, and how is it paid? There is no doubt that the most satisfactory method is for the clergy to make a regular return or 'claim' (monthly or quarterly) of all expenses, including car mileage, which is then presented to the treasurer for authentication and reimbursement. The Central Stipends Authority strongly advises this procedure, and it has drawn up a recommended claim form to be adapted for use by individual dioceses (this is reproduced as Appendix 2 at the end of this book, pp. 100–1). The use of this form is helpful as a basis for discussion between clergy and PCC officials as to what proportion of items like telephone, motoring, and hospitality is properly attributable to the parish and which to the private life of the minister concerned. If the problem of reimbursement is to be tackled effectively, it is extremely important that there should be a large measure of agreement and understanding between the clergy and the PCC.

If the idea of regular claims of actual expenditure does not commend itself, then it may have to be that the PCC simply agrees a lump sum which it pays to the clergy by monthly or quarterly instalments. This is easy to arrange, cuts down paper work, and means that the treasurer knows precisely what his outgoings are to be. On the other hand, it is imprecise, it does not relate actual payments to actual expenses, and it is easy to let the payments remain unchanged year after year whilst inflation makes them worth less and less.

What has been said about the expenses incurred by the incumbent must also apply for team vicars and assistant staff. A watch should also be kept on the expenses of clergy pensioners, non-stipendiary ministers and of people such as choirmasters, Sunday school teachers and youth leaders. The fact that they may be volunteers and enthusiasts should not stop the parish from paying for the books and equipment they need for doing their work properly. If they don't want to be paid, they can give the money back. Otherwise the prospect of taking on an expensive piece of work may deter the 'right' person from accepting the job when it next becomes vacant, and that would be unfortunate.

The reimbursement of working expenses in a team ministry will be similar to the procedures in an ordinary parish, though there may be more persons involved. Where, however, a team ministry serves two or more centres of worship which may have independent accounting systems, it is vitally necessary that the clergy and staff have a clear understanding with the parish treasurer, district or assistant treasurer(s), PCC and district church council(s) as to the extent of reimbursement. Otherwise, one might find one church within the team being more (or less) generous than the other(s). It might even be wise to have a central pool account for expenses, to which each church contributes on an agreed basis (such as by a proportion of its total income) and from which the whole team may draw as required. There are no clear-cut guidelines, but, for the sake of all concerned, there ought to be wide-ranging discussion and agreement.

In a group ministry, where there are separate parishes and separate PCCs, it may be found necessary to have inter-parochial discussions to try to reach a uniform group policy about expenses. There could, as in a team, even be a common pool to pay such items as working expenses, especially in groups where the staff work across parochial boundaries. The Church Commissioners, acting as Central Stipends Authority, in 1986 issued a revision of their booklet entitled *The Parochial Expenses of the Clergy*, specifically designed to help discussions between clergy and their parochial officers. Copies are available from 1 Millbank, free on request.

The organist

Canon B20 (1) states that:

> In all churches and chapels, other than in cathedral or collegiate churches or chapels where the matter is governed by or dependent upon the statutes or customs of the same, the functions of appointing any organist or choirmaster (by whatever name called), and of terminating the appointment of any organist or choirmaster, shall be exercisable by the minister with the agreement of the parochial church council, except that if the archdeacon of the archdeaconry in which the parish is situated, in the case of termination of an appointment, considers that the circumstances are such that the requirement as to the agreement of the parochial church council should be dispensed with, the archdeacon may

direct accordingly. Where the minister is also the archdeacon of the archdeaconry concerned, the function of the archdeacon under this paragraph shall be exercisable by the bishop of the diocese.

The actual duties carried out by organists and choirmasters vary a good deal from parish to parish, and the demands made on the time and skill of an organist in one parish may be considerably greater than those made in another. The amounts to be included in any particular parochial budget, therefore, also vary from parish to parish.

The Royal School of Church Music strongly recommends that there be a written agreement with the organist or choirmaster, and there is a form for this purpose which has been prepared by the Royal College of Organists. Copies may be obtained from RSCM for a small fee (in 1991, £1.25 including postage). Where an organist has to travel some distance between home and church, the PCC may wish to help towards the expenses incurred. The RSCM's advice about salary is that the organist of a small village or suburban church with no choir and simple services should be offered £1,000 per annum, plus £15 per wedding or funeral. (These figures are for 1991, so inflation since then should be taken into account when fixing a figure today.) For a larger village or suburban church, having a choir which rehearses once a week and sings simple anthems, the salary should be £1,250 per annum, plus £20 per wedding or funeral; and for a town church with two rehearsals weekly and regular anthems and/or settings at services, £1,750 per annum, £25 per wedding or funeral.

Payments of choristers is a matter for local decision. Some parishes regard the choir as a purely voluntary effort, others honour the long established custom whereby boys and girls are paid, perhaps according to the number of attendances.

The Incorporated Society of Musicians publishes a booklet, *Organists' Guide to Employment*, prepared by the Joint Committee of representatives of the Cathedral Organists' Association, the Incorporated Society of Musicians, the Royal College of Organists, and the Royal School of Church Music. The *Guide* (1990 edition, price £5 from ISM, RCO, or RSCM – addresses on p. 119 below) contains much helpful information about terms of contract, minimum salaries and fees for both professional and amateur organists and choir directors, broadcasting fees, performers' rights, copyright, part-time employment, private teaching and business matters.

The verger

If a verger is employed to take care of the interior of the church, whether full or part time, 'he is the servant of the persons employing him, who should be the parochial church council. It is desirable that there should be a written contract containing the terms of the employment, and the conditions on which it may be terminated by either side.'[1]

Being a servant of the Church, he will have to be paid by the PCC treasurer, so provision for such payment will have to be included in the parish budget. The extent of his work, and whether it includes work in the parish hall or other building, will be detailed in a contract of employment. A model contract, with explanatory notes, has been drawn up by the Central Board of Finance.

The parish clerk and sexton

Under Section 7(iii) of the Parochial Church Councils (Powers) Measure 1956, the power to appoint and dismiss the parish clerk and sexton, or any other person performing or assisting to perform the duties of parish clerk or sexton, and to determine their salaries and the conditions of the tenure of their offices or of their employment, is vested jointly in the parochial church council and the minister.

Tax and insurance

Wherever the PCC is responsible for the payment of wages or salaries of any employee, whether whole-time or part-time, it is subject to all the appropriate national legislation relating to PAYE, National Insurance, redundancy payments, unfair dismissal, Health and Safety at Work regulations, etc. If a treasurer is uncertain whether tax or NI contributions have to be paid, or on any other related matter, he should make enquiry of the local departments of the Inland Revenue or Department of Social Security for information.

Any persons whom the PCC employs (either part-time or whole-time) need to be insured against accident and against third-party liability, and a certificate to the effect that such insurance has been taken out has to be exhibited where the employees may read it. The cost of such insurance is generally low, and the Ecclesiastical Insurance Group will gladly advise (for address see p. 119). See also p. 53 below.

---

[1] *Handbook for Churchwardens* (1989 edition), p. 77.

3

Parochial Finances and the Wider Church

'I am the Vine', said Jesus (John 15.5), 'you are the branches.' The Church is a spiritual organism, and its life comes from its Lord. Christians are not Christians on their own. Nor are parishes; there is a wider body within which they are upheld. This family of the Church needs organizational and financial structure, so let us see how the parish fits into the wider picture.

The various levels can be shown in a diagram as follows; the first column gives the unit and the second gives the title of the 'person in charge':

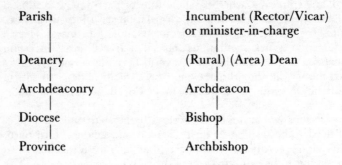

Parish	Incumbent (Rector/Vicar) or minister-in-charge
Deanery	(Rural) (Area) Dean
Archdeaconry	Archdeacon
Diocese	Bishop
Province	Archbishop

The story can go on from there, of course, like those addresses we used to put in our books when we were children, ending up with 'England, Europe, the World, the Universe, Space'. The Church of England consists of two provinces of Canterbury and York, and is itself part of the world-wide Anglican Communion of churches. For most purposes, though, the treasurer will be concerned (beyond the parish) with finance at the level of deanery, diocese, and the wider Church. The financial structures can be summarized like this:

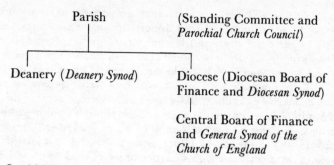

In this diagram, the bodies printed in ordinary type make financial recommendations or decisions, but those in *italics* are the ones which give final approval to budgets. In some dioceses, the financial link for assessment and payment of the diocesan share or quota is through the deanery rather than direct from diocese to parish.

There are parishes who believe that 'the diocese' or 'the centre' is something which is for ever asking for money for 'the quota' (or whatever it is called in any particular diocese), and that nothing comes back. It *is* possible to be more wrong than this – but not easily. In fact, the relation between parish and central agencies is a two-way process. A proportion of the parish minister's stipend is found centrally (by the Church Commissioners). The same is true of the costs of training before ordination (and in-service training), housing (provision and repair), pension and the 'employer's' NI contribution. Church schools are largely financed by Government or other central funds. The diocesan office and its staff and many specialist departments of the diocesan manpower are at the service of the parishes. Many dioceses give financial help towards the repair of churches and other properties in church ownership; they also advise through such departments as stewardship, religious education, social responsibility, mission and evangelism. Let us look at the way the deanery, diocesan, and national finances impinge upon the work of the parish and its treasurer.

Deanery finance

A rural deanery is a grouping of parishes (the adjective 'rural' is often quietly dropped; it hardly applies in, for example, Bermondsey, Tower Hamlets, or Bootle). The rural dean is usually one of the incumbents, who represents them and their parishes to the archdeacon or bishop.

No two deaneries are alike, because each deanery is free to choose its own financial pattern. There may be some deaneries which still work entirely on unpaid help and have no deanery budget, but most have at least a small budget to which they ask parishes to contribute according to some locally agreed apportionment. This meets the expenses of the rural dean and lay officials of the deanery. Other deaneries are more ambitious. Some may co-ordinate such projects as lay training or youth work within the deanery. Others may make financial help available to a parish which is facing a temporary crisis. A deanery might undertake evangelistic outreach or commission a study of some particular aspect of the Church's work within its borders. In some towns there may be a lay worker or minister licensed to the rural dean, either with a 'roving commission' throughout the deanery or with a particular job of work to do which the deanery supports as a corporate venture (sometimes with the assistance of the other Churches; at least one Council of Churches whose area is co-terminous with a deanery supports its own, ecumenical, full-time social responsibility officer).

Every parish in the deanery is represented on the deanery synod, and it is for the synod (often through its standing committee in the first place, though the final decision must rest with the synod as a whole) to work out its needs, prepare its budget, decide on its method of apportionment, and let the parishes know how much they are expected to contribute and by what dates.

Diocesan finances

There are 44 ways of drawing up a diocesan budget in the Church of England, corresponding to the 44 dioceses. Nevertheless, there are certain common items, though the names by which they are known will differ from diocese to diocese. Two examples are training for the ministry (or the ordination candidates' fund) and clergy stipends (or the ministry, ministerial fund, stipends fund or clergy maintenance).

These two items, in fact, account for a substantial chunk of most diocesan budgets. Although lay people are taking an increasing share in the work of the Church at all levels, and although the Church could not carry on its work without a great deal of part-time and volunteer help, it is still true that it is the ordained person around whom the teaching, pastoral and administrative work of the parish revolves; he must be adequately trained, adequately paid, and properly housed. Ministry is at the heart of the Church's structures, and manpower – people, as contrasted with offices, administration, and buildings – comes high on every church budget, whether it be parochial, diocesan or national.

What other items come on to a diocesan budget? The Diocesan Board of Education looks after the interests of church schools, as well as providing training in children's work, youth work, and adult religious education. There may be diocesan grants to supplement the pensions of clergy widows, particularly if there are orphan children to be provided for. Most dioceses have group assurance schemes to provide cash for dependants if a clergyman dies in office. Retreat houses are usually subsidized by the diocese. Some dioceses make grants to help in the repair of church buildings. There is social responsibility work, especially in the fields of family welfare and adoption. Many dioceses run in-service training courses for ordained and full-time lay staff. There is also a diocesan office in every diocese, with a diocesan secretary. Through that office, advice may be obtained on a wide number of administrative matters affecting the parishes and their relations with the diocese, with General Synod, and with the Church Commissioners. Then there are the expenses of diocesan officials (car, telephone, offices) and the costs of sending the representatives of the diocese to General Synod three times a year.

The diocesan office is usually the registered office of the Diocesan Board of Finance – usually a registered company, which has charitable status. The DBF is named in measures of the General Synod as the 'diocesan authority', and we will have more to say about that function of the DBF when we come to matters affecting parish property.

The diocesan budget is built up by the DBF after asking the various diocesan boards and committees for estimates of what they expect to require in the year ahead. The DBF will also have received information from the Central Board of Finance(see the next section) about the amount needed from the diocese towards the running of General Synod. The Church Commissioners (acting as Central Stipends Authority) will have informed the DBF about recommended stipend levels for the year ahead and about the sum available from them towards meeting increases in the stipends of ministers and lay workers within the diocese. All these figures are carefully perused and discussed (often not only by the DBF but by the boards and committees concerned, and by deanery and parish bodies too) and finally presented to the Diocesan Synod.

When the Synod accepts the budget, it also decides how to apportion the total sum amongst the deaneries or parishes. Each diocese has its own method of apportionment. Some are based on the actual income of the parishes either for the last year or averaged over the previous few years, but more and more are coming round to an assessment for the 'quota' or 'share' based on a mutually agreed figure of 'parish potential'. Some dioceses allow each parish the first *x* hundred pounds of parish income (or potential) free of quota, or they may exempt missionary and charitable giving. Some use a fixed percentage, others adopt a sliding scale. There are 44 variations on a theme.

Has the 'person in the pew' got any say in all this? Of course. Lay persons are in the majority on every parochial church council, usually in the majority on the Deanery Synod, and have equal representation with the clergy on the Diocesan Synod and General Synod. Any communicant whose name is on the parish electoral roll can stand for election to the PCC or other bodies, and can make his voice heard. It is important that the Church's synods should never become remote bodies, out of touch with lay opinion at parish level.

The Central Board of Finance

The CBF (the Central Board of Finance of the Church of England) is incorporated under the Companies Acts as the financial executive of the General Synod and is also trustee for certain central funds of the Church of England. The General Synod appoints its boards, councils, committees, and commissions, and it is the responsibility of the CBF to ascertain their needs, scrutinize their expenditure, and prepare a budget for the consideration of General Synod. As in the diocese, however, the final authority for accepting a budget and for apportioning it lies with the Synod itself.

Since 1984, the General Synod Apportionment has been based partly on income from dioceses and parishes, and partly on potential factors, reflecting the wide use of potential in parochial quota/share schemes of individual dioceses. The formula is briefly described in the CBF's Annual Report. This is why the CBF needs to know the income of every parish in the Church of England, and one reason why returns of parochial income have to be prepared and submitted. The CBF's Statistical Unit is responsible for collecting and collating all this information, which is of much wider use than purely financial – it helps in the long-term planning of the whole of the Church of England.

The CBF's Annual Report gives a brief description of the current General Synod Apportionment Scheme. Broadly speaking, it includes all cash collections and envelope schemes, tax recovered from deeds of covenant, interest on investments, net proceeds of letting the parish hall, rents, and income from trust funds. Deductions are allowed only in the case of grants made for stipends of clergy and lay workers. The parish treasurer may baulk at the detail which is required in the return of parish income; but unless the figures are known, it is not possible to make a fair apportionment of the General Synod budget (which for 1992 came to around thirteen million pounds).

This budget includes the cost of training men and women for the full-time ministry, the finances necessary for the boards and committees of the General Synod, and contributions to such bodies as the Anglican Consultative Council, the Lambeth Conference, the World Council of Churches, and other (national and international) ecumenical bodies. There is also the chaplaincy work in modern universities and polytechnics. Each year the CBF produces its Annual Report, which is sent to every General Synod member, and which may be obtained from the Secretary to the Board at Church House, Westminster.

The CBF also has an Investment Office in the City. This was set up in 1958 to manage funds under the Church Funds Investment Measure 1958 by the Church Assembly (the predecessor of the General Synod). It offers investment facilities to churches and dioceses through an Investment Fund, Fixed Interest Securities Fund, and Deposit Fund. Your diocesan office or the Investment Office itself will always be glad to give information or advice about whether to invest parochial moneys in any of these funds; they provide the Church with continuous professional investment management of a high quality. The broad characteristics of the three funds are as follows:

The Investment Fund

This is only suitable for long-term investment, and offers continuing investment management through a mixed fund with a flexible investment policy. Its portfolio is primarily invested in equities, at home and overseas, but it also has a proportion invested in real property and fixed-interest securities. It aims to provide a steady growth in income over the years and provide protection against inflation for the capital invested.

The Fixed Interest Securities Fund

This (invested, as its name implies, mainly in fixed interest securities) is suitable only for the investment of that portion of long-term capital on which it is essential to obtain an immediate high yield. It should be recognized that Fixed Interest Securities offer little protection against inflation for income and capital. This fund is intended to supplement, where necessary, the main CBF Investment Fund.

Both the Investment and Fixed Interest Securities Funds are valued at the end of each month, and contributions and withdrawals can be made on any valuation date.

The Deposit Fund

This is more flexible, and can be used for the deposit of large or small amounts of money which can be withdrawn on demand without capital loss – but also, without capital gain. By grouping money together, the fund can obtain more favourable interest rates in the money market than can be obtained for smaller sums. Deposits can be made at any time. The rate of interest is calculated daily and paid quarterly.

All money paid into any of these three funds must be held on charitable trusts, whose objects have to be shown to be 'connected with the Church of England'. The funds are exempt from liability to tax on either income or capital gains owing to their charitable status. Dividends and interest are paid gross. They can thus be used by dioceses, deaneries, and parishes, but not for the investment of money belonging to individuals.

The Church Commissioners

In 1948, the Church Commissioners were formed from an amalgamation of the Ecclesiastical Commissioners and Queen Anne's Bounty. They inherited from their predecessors

> a General Fund, derived partly from the Corporate Fund of QAB, which was held upon trust to augment the incomes of the poorer beneficed clergy, and partly from the much larger Common Fund of the Ecclesiastical Commissioners, held upon trust to make additional provision for 'the cure of souls' (or in more modern language 'pastoral supervision') in parishes where such assistance was most required, in such manner as should be deemed most conducive to the efficiency of the Established Church.[1]

It is still a major responsibility of the Church Commissioners to make available as much money as possible for paying the stipends and pensions of the clergy and full-time lay workers – i.e. those engaged in the 'cure of souls'. We have already mentioned (p. 25) the money they make available towards stipends. In 1990, 80 per cent of the Commissioners' income was used for the payment of ordained and lay staff engaged in the cure of souls in dioceses and parishes, for pensions for the clergy and their widows, and for clergy housing.

As far as buildings are concerned, the Commissioners make large sums of money available to the dioceses for the repair, improvement, decoration, building, and buying of parsonage houses. In some dioceses the parishes are asked by the diocese to be partners with the Commissioners in this, so that the Commissioners' money may go

---

[1] *The First Five Years – the Story of the Church Commissioners 1948–53*, Sir Philip Baker Wilbraham (First Church Estates Commissioner 1939–54). Published for the Church Commissioners by SPCK, 1953.

further. Since 1945, the Commissioners have also released large sums of money for new buildings (churches, halls and houses) in new housing areas, often by way of making money available to supplement what has been raised locally.

Despite shrewd policies of investment and reinvestment, the large sums of money which the Commissioners administer are not sufficient in an inflationary age to meet all the calls upon them. It therefore falls to the dioceses to find an increasingly large percentage of the extra money for stipends, and to pay more and more towards the cost of providing and maintaining parsonages. This in turn means bigger and bigger requests to the parishes, for few dioceses have much accumulated funds 'salted away'. Parishes may groan, but if it were not for the Church Commissioners, the sums requested would be even larger; and if they could not be met, then churches would have to do without their full-time paid ministers.

Having said this, it is – splendidly – true that lay people and PCCs have responded well to a changing financial situation. The fact that an increasing proportion of the cost of maintaining the ministry has fallen upon the congregation of the faithful, does not seem to have dismayed them. It used to be said that, if the clergy were to spend their time in proportion to the sources of their income, they would be in the graveyard six days a week and with their congregations only for an hour or so on Sunday. That gibe is no longer true, thank God.

The Pensions Board

Pensions for clergy, deaconesses and licensed lay workers are non-contributory. The Church of England Pensions Board keeps the records for pensions purposes, calculates the amounts payable, and undertakes a great deal of administrative and committee work in connection with pensions. The pensions themselves, and the lump sums paid on retirement, are paid by the Church Commissioners in accordance with the Church of England (Pensions) Measures 1961–88. The Pensions Board administers moneys for survivorship pensions for widows, grants in augmentation of pensions (where needed) in partnership with the dioceses, and the Church Workers' Pension Fund (for lay workers). Church lay workers, such as diocesan office staff and family welfare workers, may join this Pension Fund on a contributory basis. In some such cases the employer (Diocesan Board of Finance, Diocesan Family Welfare Council, etc.) voluntarily pays the employee's contribution as well as that due from the employer.

The Pensions Board, with financial assistance from the Church Commissioners, is responsible for housing the retired clergy, deaconesses, and licensed lay workers and their widows/widowers. Applicants with reasonable capital are expected to purchase their own accommodation with the aid of an equity sharing mortgage, and such finance is available from the age of 57. Those who cannot afford to purchase their own properties will be eligible for rented accommodation when they retire.

Nursing and residential accommodation is available in various homes owned by the Pensions Board. The running costs for these homes is met from the fees paid by residents and patients and from the Board's charitable funds.

As with the Church Commissioners, the Board also finds that its funds are insufficient. Subscriptions, donations, legacies, and bequests are needed now more than ever for homes for retired clergy, their widows, and retired church workers. Many parish treasurers therefore will find an item for the Pensions Board on their budget or on their list of charitable giving.

The Annual Report of the Board is distributed to General Synod members and is available on request from the Pensions Board at 7 Little College Street, London SW1P 3SF. The Board's staff are always ready to answer queries or give guidance.

4

Property and Trust Funds

In this chapter, we deal only with those aspects of parish property which may be the concern of the treasurer.

All sorts of buildings and land could loosely be referred to as 'parish property', but the legal ownership and financial liability are not as simple as that. Ownership does not necessarily define where the financial liability for upkeep and maintenance lies. In nearly all cases, whilst the PCC may not be the owner, it has the responsibility of upkeep – sometimes a legal responsibility, sometimes a moral responsibility based upon custom. The PCC treasurer, therefore, needs to know the extent of his council's liabilities.

The terrier and inventory

A 'terrier' is an account of the territory and possessions of the church. Canon F17 requires that 'a full note and terrier of all lands, goods and other possessions of the parochial churches and chapels therein be compiled and kept by the minister and churchwardens', and instructs the archdeacon (or the rural dean acting on his behalf) to check every three years that this has been done.

The terrier should list the lands and buildings belonging to the church – except for glebe, for which see p. 32 below. This will include the church, churchyard, all unconsecrated buildings which are parochial assets such as a curate's or verger's house, church hall, etc.; and will include a schedule of benefactions and trusts connected with the church. It should not, however, contain details of the movable property within the church building. This should be listed in the inventory, which should be as full a record as possible of the contents of the building. This is to be kept by the churchwardens (according to Canon E1) and handed over to their successors whenever there is a change of churchwarden. Really valuable items such as plate and altar ornaments should be photographed as a help to the police should there ever be a theft. The inventory should not list prayer and hymn books, baptism cards and other ephemera subject to wear and tear and needing constant replacement.

The Church Information Office publish a combined Terrier and Inventory as a large-size 32-page volume. This form of record was authorized by General Synod in 1972, and copies can be bought at Church House Bookshop, or ordered from the local SPCK. When compiled, it should be kept in the church safe with other important documents and registers.

Parish Log Book

The companion to the Terrier and Inventory is the Parish Log Book. Canon F13 (4) provides that 'a record of all alterations, removals, or repairs so executed shall be kept in a book to be provided for the purpose and the record shall indicate where specifications and plans may be inspected if not deposited with the book'. New (loose-leaf) log books are published by CIO and may be bought from the Church House Bookshop. The Log Book should also contain a summary of the architect's quinquennial report on the church fabric and details of such items as insurance cover and amounts of money set aside each year for repairs. A properly kept Log Book provides in one document a factual record of church repairs, restoration work, insurance cover, and fabric fund. It is not, strictly speaking, a financial document, but the church treasurer will examine it with interest to see what his likely liabilities might be over the next few years in respect of the church building. It is also a useful document for anyone wishing to write the history of the parish, for it will show at a glance what has been happening to the church building over a number of years, and the cost.

Glebe

Until 1978, when the Endowments and Glebe Measure 1976 came into operation, glebe land and buildings were part of the benefice property (see p. 6 above) and belonged to the incumbent for the time being by virtue of his office. The rents therefore formed part of his benefice income and did not belong to the PCC. Now, glebe has come into diocesan ownership and is administered for the benefit of the Diocesan Stipends Fund as a whole. The PCC treasurer should not, therefore, need to be involved with questions on glebe.

There are two borderline cases. (1) If the parsonage house has been divided by a formal and permanent division, then that part of the house where the incumbent lives remains a benefice house (for which see pp. 38–9 below) and the part which has been divided off from it will be glebe. The diocesan office should have a certificate with a plan showing the line of division. If there is not a copy of the plan with the terrier, it would be an advantage to have a photocopy made. Then it is readily available in the parish in case of any doubts about which part of the house and garden is which, and who is responsible for any shared accesses or party walls. (2) Similarly, if the parsonage garden and glebe field are adjacent, a plan should be kept with the terrier showing where the boundary lies and who has to maintain which walls and hedges.

If the PCC owns land, this is not glebe land but PCC land, and the foregoing comments do not apply.

The church building

The freehold of a consecrated parish church vests in the incumbent, but it is held by him for the use of parishioners, the management being vested on their behalf in the incumbent, the churchwardens and the PCC. Possession is with the incumbent and churchwardens jointly. The legal ownership of the movable furniture and ornaments vests in the churchwardens. Despite all this, the financial responsibility for the building and its contents lies entirely with the PCC (unless there is a lay rector still responsible for repairs to the chancel, or family aisles or chantries belonging to an ancient family connected with the parish, when there may be an exception).

The Inspection of Churches Measure 1955 provides that every consecrated church shall be inspected by a qualified person every five years, and he should make a report on the condition of its fabric. The cost of this inspection falls on the PCC, though different dioceses have varying ways of collecting it. Some dioceses operate a scheme whereby the cost is included within the diocesan budget and is paid for as part of the parish share or quota. In others, it is up to the parish to make its own arrangements with the architect. In such cases, the fee should be agreed in advance, and the wise parish will put aside a sum each year so that the whole amount does not have to come out of a single year's budget.

Although the financial responsibility for the upkeep and repair of the church building belongs to the PCC, neither the PCC nor the wardens nor the incumbent are free to do just as they wish with the building without further consultation and consents. The building is held on trust for the parishioners, and parishioners' interests must be safeguarded if there are any proposals to alter the building or add to it. This is done through the faculty jurisdiction, under the chancellor of the diocese, who also exercises authority over work on the curtilage of the church. Minor matters need the authorization of the archdeacon; other proposals must have the chancellor's faculty. Application is made – not direct either to the archdeacon or the chancellor – but through the registrar of the diocese. The chancellor is advised by the Diocesan Advisory Committee for the Care of Churches (the DAC). The DAC will also give advice to parishes when proposals are being discussed and formulated. It is as well to be in touch with the DAC secretary at as early a stage as possible, whilst plans are still fluid enough to be modified as a result of listening to the DAC's advice. It would be irresponsible to pay fees to architects and/or designers, have plans made or place orders for ornaments, and then discover that the proposals did not have the support of the DAC, or that the chancellor was not prepared to issue a faculty. The treasurer should bear this in mind and always ask the PCC and incumbent questions about grant of faculty or certificate whenever there are proposals involving the faculty jurisdiction.

Faculty jurisdiction applies to all consecrated churches, and to many which are dedicated, not consecrated. If your church is only dedicated, the DAC secretary can inform you as to its position with regard to faculty jurisdiction. He (or your archdeacon) will also be able to advise about possible sources of grants or loans in aid of the work. Some dioceses administer funds which can be used for this; there are many (local or national) charities which may help; and if your church is of architectural or historic importance, or in a conservation area, it may qualify for a grant from English Heritage under the scheme of state aid for historic churches in use. Application for this last can only be made through your archdeacon, and no grant will be paid if the work has been begun before the grant has been approved.

Some daughter (or mission) churches, and some modern parish churches or church buildings in conventional districts, may not have been consecrated, and may vest in the Diocesan Board of Finance. In this case, the powers of management will usually rest with the PCC, but the division of functions between ownership and management should be clear in the original deed. If, however, a mission church was in use prior to the Parochial Church Councils (Powers) Measure first becoming law in 1921, the legal interest in it may have been vested either in the incumbent and churchwardens or in the Official Custodian for Charities. If that is the case, even if action has been taken under the Incumbents and Churchwardens (Trusts) Measure 1964, the PCC still has no legal rights (or legally enforceable financial responsibilities). If the parish has, however, been maintaining the property it would be morally right to continue to do so, if it is fully recognized that it is not PCC property, and that any proceeds of sale will not legally belong to the PCC.

The churchyard

The legal ownership of a churchyard is normally vested in the incumbent, and he receives certain fees for allowing monuments to be erected, and for burials in it if the churchyard is still open for burials. Plots in the churchyard may only be reserved for named persons under the authority of the chancellor's faculty. The person who pays a fee does not thereby become the owner of the land in question, nor does he become legally responsible for the upkeep of that plot of land. All he has been granted is permission to bury, or to erect a monument.

As well as fees to the incumbent in these cases, there are fees payable to the PCC, and these can be used to offset the cost of maintenance of the churchyard. If the churchyard has been closed for burials by an Order in Council under the Burial Acts, the PCC may make a written request to the Local Authority for the authority to be responsible for its maintenance (including walls, fences, and boundaries). Three months after submission of the request, the responsibility then statutorily passes to the Local Authority. The ownership of the churchyard is not affected, and the Local Authority must obtain faculty authorization for any works it proposes to do, such as removal of kerbs or gravestones or landscaping. Even if a churchyard has not been closed by Order in Council, a local authority is empowered under the Open Spaces Acts to make a voluntary contribution towards churchyard maintenance, and this is always worth trying.

The closure of churchyards is a complex matter; any PCC contemplating it should first get in touch either with the secretary of the Diocesan Advisory Committee, the archdeacon or the diocesan registrar for advice. See also p. 143 (and note 3) of *A Handbook for Churchwardens and Parochial Church Councillors* (1989 edition).

Parish halls: Housing for parish staff

The parish hall, and all housing for the clergy and lay staff for whom 'parish' housing is provided, will be held on charitable trusts. Before the Parochial Church Councils (Powers) Measure 1921, this type of church property was vested in the names of individuals – more often than not, the incumbent and churchwardens. Where they were named as individuals rather than as the holders of the office for the time being, it did not necessarily follow that their successors in office became trustees in turn. Frequently, with the death of the last survivor of the original trustees, no steps were taken to ensure the appointment of new trustees. In this case it may become necessary to apply to the Charity Commissioners to remedy the situation.

In those cases where properties were vested in the incumbent and churchwardens, the provisions of the Incumbents and Churchwardens (Trusts) Measure 1964 can prove very useful. In every case of doubt the incumbent and churchwardens concerned should consult the Diocesan Board of Finance who, if the Measure applies, can assist by having the property vested in the Board, leaving the powers of management with the incumbent and churchwardens for the time being. In those cases where, in practice, the PCC is acting as managing trustee and is financially responsible for the property, the Charity Commissioners may, with the consent of the incumbent and churchwardens, issue a Scheme regularizing the position and naming the PCC as managing trustee.

Properties (halls, curates' houses, vergers' cottages etc.) acquired since 1921 which are held on permanent trusts fall to be dealt with under the Parochial Church Councils (Powers) Measure 1956. This Measure is set out, with notes, on pp. 139–57 of *A Handbook for Churchwardens and Parochial Church Councillors* (1989 edition – for details see p. 117 below). Under section 5 of the Measure, a PCC has power to acquire any property, real or personal (whether by way of gift or purchase or otherwise) for any ecclesiastical purpose affecting the parish or any part of it. It also has power to manage, administer and dispose of any property acquired. Section 6 provides that if a PCC holds or acquires an interest in land (other than a short lease, for a term of a year or less) or any interest in personal property to be held on permanent trusts, such interest shall be vested in the diocesan authority (i.e. the DBF); but the PCC must indemnify the DBF in respect of all liabilities to the property (e.g. water rate, taxes, insurance premium, legal charges, upkeep and maintenance costs, repair bills etc.). In other words, the DBF is the bare holding trustee or custodian trustee, whilst the PCC is the managing trustee, with all the duties which this status implies.

If the PCC decides that it has no further use for a particular property and that it would be beneficial to have it sold, then the PCC should consult with the DBF as to the proper method of achieving this. The steps to be taken are not necessarily the same in each case, but the DBF will advise as to what is required in each particular instance. It is, of course, important to remember that the proceeds of sale are in many cases to be treated as capital moneys and cannot be made available to the PCC for its general purposes. Any use of the capital as opposed to the income will probably require the approval of, and be subject to, the conditions laid down by the Charity Commissioners. It is impossible to give general advice, as title deeds and trusts vary so widely. Legal experts must be consulted, and the DBF solicitor will probably be helpful.

Often, the proceeds of sale have to be put in trust as capital, and only the interest arising from them can be used by the PCC. Sometimes the trust is an ancient one and its original purpose may be incapable of fulfilment. If so, the Charity Commissioners will have to make a Scheme whereby the funds can be administered in a way which approximates as closely as possible to the presumed wishes of those who set up the original trust in the first place.

A particular snag hits parishes which decide to sell their 'church hall' only to find, on examining the title deeds, that the property was originally established on an educational trust – possibly for use as a day school in the days before universal State education. When this happens the Charity Commissioners will become involved. In general terms, these properties remain subject to educational trusts as opposed to ecclesiastical trusts. If a parish has a so-called 'church hall' which is held on educational trusts, and wishes to retain it as a church hall, it may be possible for the PCC to 'buy out' the educational trust, and create an ecclesiastical trust. In these cases, advice should be sought from the Diocesan Director of Education or the Secretary of the DBF, and the DBF's solicitor will probably also need to help with advice as to the legal position. Until such time as this advice has been obtained, the PCC would be well advised not to spend any parochial moneys on capital works.

All this information about the trusts upon which church property is held ought to be recorded in the parish terrier, but this is not always the case, and many a parish has had a nasty shock when it thought it was selling its old parish hall and found when it did so that it was trying to sell property not in its legal ownership (see p. 43).

When a PCC-owned house becomes vacant, expert legal advice should be sought before letting it. It is tempting to try to make a few pounds on a 'temporary' let; but the Rent Acts give such protection to tenants that it may be quite impossible to regain possession of the property when it is needed again for its original purpose. There does not need to be a formal agreement, or a rent book, for a tenancy to be created; even letting at a sub-economic rent as a concession will not protect the PCC's interest. If the house is in an area prone to vandalism, and the PCC wants to protect its property, the best way to do so may not be to let it out to rent, but to 'employ' a family as 'caretakers' at a wage of 10p per month and to require them to live in the house as a condition of their employment. In such a case, what is created is a 'service' tenancy which can be terminated when the house is needed again. Or the property can be let furnished, or subject to a shorthold tenancy, which in both cases gives the tenants fewer rights than in the case of unfurnished tenancies. But the whole subject bristles with snags, and a solicitor should be asked to advise. What is certain is that if a tenant comes into a house, and is unwilling to move, and the PCC then decides to cut its losses and sell the house and buy another, it will find itself very much the poorer. Sale prices subject to an existing tenancy are much less than 'with vacant possession'.

Parsonage houses

Most incumbents' houses (rectories and vicarages, but not houses occupied by ministers-in-charge of conventional districts) are benefice property. This means they are vested in the incumbent by virtue of his office. Occasionally, a parsonage house is an 'unofficial' one and may be vested in the DBF as holding trustee with the PCC as managing trustee. This state of affairs may arise because the Commissioners will not normally accept a house as the official benefice house unless it measures up to certain standards (mainly relating to the number and size of its rooms). More often it is because the house is owned by a trust.

The Church Commissioners make grants available towards decoration and improvement of official parsonage houses and the houses of team vicars. The Commissioners also contribute, through Diocesan Parsonage Boards, for the repairs, water rate and other outgoings of incumbents' houses, whether or not these are official parsonages. The Commissioners' help is always given via the Diocesan Parsonages Board or Committee (the romantic old title of Dilapidations Board, redolent of the crumbling ruins of Barchester, was done away with in the 1970s).

Every five years, the parsonage house is inspected by the diocesan surveyor, who issues a schedule of necessary repair work; this (and the exterior redecoration which counts as a repair for these purposes) should be put in hand in accordance with the diocesan scheme established under the Repair of Benefice Buildings Measure 1972. Most diocesan schemes require an annual payment from each parish towards the repair, exterior redecoration, and insurance of the parsonage, and then the diocese pays the cost of agreed repairs out of the Parsonages Fund into which the parochial contributions (and Commissioners' grants etc.) are fed. But each diocese has its own variations. What is certain is that the PCC treasurer will need to set aside money in each year's budget towards water rate and parsonage repair costs, though in many dioceses the payment may be merged in the general quota/share paid to the diocese.

The diocesan insurance only covers the fabric of the parsonage house; it is for the incumbent himself to take out such insurance as he wishes to cover damage to, or loss of, its contents. Some PCCs may wish to help their incumbent with the cost of doing so (see also p. 55 below).

Interior decoration does not count as part of the quinquennial repair (unless it is redecoration consequential on repair work, such as an electric rewiring operation). Diocesan Parsonage Boards have sums for interior decoration allocated to them by the Church Commissioners, but they are not large, and the way in which the funds are administered differs from diocese to diocese. A PCC ought to try to help the incumbent with the cost of interior redecoration – the parsonage house is usually bigger than the average house in the parish, and the parson's stipend may be smaller than the average wage; so the cost of keeping the house spick and span is heavy if the PCC does not do something towards it. An annual allocation, allowing (say) a couple of rooms to be done each year, is better than letting the house become so dingy that when there is a vacancy, no minister (or clergy spouse) will consent to live in it until it has been completely – and inordinately expensively – redecorated.

Any improvements to the parsonage must be approved by the Parsonages Board. The Board will usually be able to make a grant in aid, and/or a loan to enable the work to begin straight away before inflation makes it harder to pay for. The Church Commissioners' consent is also required in the case of larger improvement schemes, but the Diocesan Parsonages Board usually does all the negotiations about this.

Parsonages are benefice property, not PCC property. If they are sold, therefore, the PCC cannot take any part of the proceeds, even though it may have contributed substantially towards the initial cost and subsequent upkeep of the house. When the house is sold and a replacement one bought or built, it is usual for the proceeds of sale to go towards the cost of the new house. If there is a profit on the transaction, the Commissioners will hold it, sometimes in a special fund which can finance capital improvements, sometimes for eventual transfer to the Diocesan Stipends Fund. If a parsonage house is sold and there is no replacement, there is usually a Scheme under the Pastoral Measure 1983 which says how the sale proceeds are to be applied.

All the above applies to official parsonage houses owned by the benefice. If the parsonage is an unofficial one (generally, owned by the PCC, with the DBF acting as custodian trustee) the treasurer should check the position with the diocesan office, as it is possible that the PCC may need to make special budgetary provision towards repairs, redecoration, insurance, improvement, etc.

Church schools

A large number of parishes have church schools which, although built and maintained under educational trusts to which the PCC is not legally a party, may well look towards the PCC for financial assistance. Many PCCs will feel it right to express their support for the parish school in financial terms even though the school is administered by its own Governors and the PCC has no legal responsibility towards it.

Under the 1944 Education Act there are three distinct types of Voluntary Church Schools – Aided, Controlled and Special Agreement Schools. Each has its own particular character and relationship with the Church as set out in the terms of the 1944 Act and subsequent amending legislation. The Diocesan Board of Education will be able to help and advise, and treasurers wishing to do so should contact the Diocesan Director of Education.

In the case of Special Agreement Schools, treasurers would do best to consult the Diocesan Board of Education to discover the terms under which they operate.

The words 'controlled' and 'aided' are used from the point of view of the Local Education Authority, not from the point of view of the Church. A 'Church of England (Controlled) School' is not one controlled by the C of E, but one where the control (as represented by the majority in the Governing Body) lies with the other constituencies – i.e. with the governors elected by the LEA, parents, and teachers, and with the co-opted governors. An 'Aided' school is one where the majority of Church-appointed governors is 'aided' by a minority of elected parent and teacher governors and those appointed through the LEA.

Controlled Schools

The buildings are vested in trustees who in the case of parochial schools are usually the incumbent and churchwardens (who hold the property on educational trusts as distinct from ecclesiastical trusts). The PCC, if it wishes, may voluntarily provide resources additional to those provided by the LEA, but any financial contribution by the PCC will be purely an expression of the support and well-wishing of the local church for the work being done in the school and not a contribution to the maintenance of the school itself (compare the case of the Aided School, below). Thus some parishes may present the school-leavers with a Bible, or underwrite the cost of a visit to the cathedral. Others may wish to contribute towards some additional piece of equipment which the school requires and for which its budget is insufficient. In such a case, the offer of help should be made to the Governors. If the gift is an alteration to the structure or fitments of the building, like a set of doors or a windporch, the Governors will not be able to act without the agreement of the LEA, who will probably make the stipulation that the work shall be subject to the approval of the Authority's architect.

Aided Schools

The Church appoints the majority of the Governors (the 'Foundation Governors') in an Aided School. In the case of a primary school, one of the Foundation Governors will be the incumbent ex-officio and at least one will be nominated by the PCC. The Governors (and that generally in practice means the Foundation Governors) have to find 15 per cent of the capital cost of the building and the same percentage towards repairs and maintenance of the exterior (with the exception of the kitchens, which are wholly maintained by the LEA). The diagram on p. 173 of *County and Voluntary Schools* (see p. 117 below) is a useful 'visual aid' to show the normal division of responsibilities between LEA and Governors in the case of repairs to the Aided School building, though financial arrangements agreed between some dioceses and LEAs to implement certain provisions of the Local Management of Schools of the 1988 Education Reform Act, as they affect Aided Schools in particular, have complicated the picture. The Diocesan Director of Education should be consulted where doubts arise about the interpretation of the diagram. The remaining 85 per cent is grant aided by the Department of Education and Science. In addition the Governors usually have to insure the school building against fire and storm damage. Most LEAs, under the provisions of the Local Management of Schools, maintain insurance cover over aspects of school buildings, including contents and fittings, though Governors are free to extend the insurance cover in their schools. Questions about the apportionment of costs and the grant aid available are matters to be discussed by the Governors with the Diocesan Director of Education.

Where does the Church's 15 per cent come from? Some Aided Schools may have trust funds or the rents from properties to help the governors meet their obligations. Many dioceses run a Diocesan Maintenance Scheme (sometimes called a 'Barchester Scheme'), and negotiate a block insurance policy into which the Governors pay an agreed sum. The diocese (through its Board of Education) may make a grant towards capital expenditure, the cost of running repairs, and the general maintenance of the school. On top of this, it is usually the case that the PCC makes an annual grant to assist the Governors in the discharge of their financial responsibilities; but this is a voluntary donation – the school building belongs to the Trustees and its financial affairs are the concern of the Governors. The Governors should always have their own School Account which does not form part of the PCC accounts. The PCC may well request a copy of the Governors' Balance Sheet and Accounts when making its financial allocations for the coming year, and a PCC which makes money available to the parish school should take steps to ensure that the school is being properly maintained. It ought also to review the viability of the school from time to time in terms of pupil numbers, so that it can assess the appropriateness of continuing to make any financial contributions.

In some deaneries there may be Aided Schools which serve the deanery or a part of it rather than a single parish. This is often the case with Aided Secondary Schools, which are usually too large and too expensive to be supported by one parish unless there are massive trust funds available to the school. In these circumstances it is usual for the parochial contributions to the Deanery School to be worked out on a deanery basis, and often levied through the deanery quota/share or in some similar way.

The cost of running the school, as distinct from the maintenance and insurance of the buildings, is paid entirely by the LEA through a system involving the delegation of part of their budget to the governing body. The Governors will be responsible under the scheme of delegation for the decisions about how the budget is expended on such items as the payment of teaching staff and ancillary staff, the purchase of equipment and fittings and the heating, lighting and cleaning of the school.

Parish use of church schools

The church school does not belong to the PCC. It has its own Trust Deeds and Governing Body. The Governors do have the right to use, or allow the use of, the building out of school hours on certain days. However, this right does not mean that they can allow the PCC to have use of the premises free of charge. The Governors will expect to receive appropriate payment from all users of the school buildings and certainly the cost of heating, lighting, cleaning and caretaking will have to be covered. The Governors are responsible for ensuring the healthy balance of their budget in order to maintain efficient education in the school and thus they will expect to raise revenue from every letting, though Church groups might reasonably expect to be treated with special consideration. When compared with the cost of maintaining a church hall, for instance, the price of using the school will be seen to be very low indeed.

Closure

If a church school has been closed because it has been transferred to another site, and the old school is sold, the proceeds are usually payable to the LEA. If it is closed because it is surplus to require-ments, then unless the building reverts to the original donor (or his heirs), who will in that case be responsible for its future use, it will have to be sold and the proceeds used under the direction of the DES for other educational purposes in the diocese.

Even if the school has served the parish for many years as its parish hall, it is very rare indeed for the building automatically to become the property of the parish when the school closes. The parish, if it wants to have the building, will have to buy it from the diocese or other owner. Since the school is held on an educational trust, the diocese (or the trustees) are under a legal obligation to see that whoever buys the school pays full market value for the buildings.

This also applies to school houses, which once would have been the home of the head teacher and might have been used by the parish for a number of years to house a verger or assistant clergy. In most cases these will prove to be part of the educational endowment and will be treated in the same way as the school building itself.

The legal complexities are numerous, so be sure to consult the Diocesan Director of Education, the Secretary of the DBF or the Board's Solicitor (see p. 37).

General

Treasurers with problems over church schools should contact the Diocesan Director of Education.

Development Land Tax

Charities are exempt from the payment of Development Land Tax as from March 1980.

Local Government Finance

The rating of trust property became less complex in April 1990, but the arrival of the community charge has thrown up new problems.

General

The Local Government Finance Act 1988 altered the way local authorities raise income. The community charge replaced domestic rates (see below), while non-domestic properties became the subject of a new non-domestic business rate. At the time of writing, the Government has announced that the community charge is to be replaced by the so-called council tax in April 1993, although the proposals are currently very embryonic.

As the cost of domestic rates on clergy accommodation (taking account of the normal 50 per cent charitable relief) had been borne by parish or diocese, the Church stood to save around £3m. As the Government would not agree to any exemption for the clergy from meeting the personal community charge, the eventual cost to the Church was around £11.5m (or £8.5m net allowing for the saving on rates).

Some of that additional cost was offset by a package of counter-vailing benefits agreed by the Government, totalling about £3.75m per year. Most of these benefits referred to state aid for churches in use, but significant savings affect the application of the non-domestic business rate as it applies to church property.

Rates

Church buildings. From 1 April 1990, all places of public religious worship belonging to the Church of England have been exempt. This continues the practice of the previous system. (Water authorities still have the power to levy a water rate – even if there is no water supply to the building!)

Church halls. Similarly these have become exempt from 1 April 1990, regardless of whether a parish is receiving any income or not from lettings.

Parsonages and other clergy housing. Because these are regarded as domestic property, the community charge legislation applies, and the relevant bills will fall to be paid by the occupants. If a property is empty pending the arrival of a new minister, then the owner (effectively the diocese in most cases) is exempt from paying the *standard* community charge. In the few cases where a clergy house is empty pending its eventual sale, the local authority is able to levy the standard community charge.

Other church property. Generally speaking, these properties too are exempt from rates, provided they are used to support the organization of Church of England worship, such as diocesan offices, theological colleges etc. If such a property does not fall under this category, mandatory charitable relief of 80 per cent will apply, with local authorities able to waive all, or a proportion of, the remaining 20 per cent.

It is possible to appeal against a rating assessment. If the parish cannot agree with the rating valuation officer on appeal, legal advice should be obtained. The diocesan office or the archdeacon should be approached in the first instance.

The community charge

The abolition of domestic rates (a property tax) has seen the replacement by the community charge (a personal tax).

The personal community charge. Like everybody else, the clergy and their spouses have been liable to the personal charge. But unlike most, they did not have the benefit of domestic rates savings to help offset the cost. During the annual round of discussions with dioceses about future stipend levels held in 1989 (see p. 13), the majority of dioceses agreed to a considerable rise in stipends over and above the normal cost of living increase to help meet the cost of the clergy's charge liability. With substantial help from the Commissioners' investment income, this ambition was achieved in 1990 so that generally the charge liability of most clergy, including spouses, was covered.

In subsequent years, the community charge was to be considered as just one of several factors in setting stipend levels. For 1991, headline charge levels were reduced substantially in the Budget, while at the same time, the clergy have benefited from the Community Charge Relief Scheme. This has resulted in the average clergy charge bill falling by more than half the levels of 1990, and due allowance has been made in setting stipend levels.

The standard community charge. The CSA made no allowance within their stipend recommendations for clergy meeting the cost of the standard community charge, for those owning their own homes. In 1990, most local authorities made no concession for the fact that clergy lived in tied accommodation, so that most clergy were faced with a bill equivalent to two personal community charges for the appropriate local authority. After extensive lobbying, the Government announced for 1991 that for those living in tied accommodation, the standard charge could be the equivalent of no more than one-half the personal charge.

The council tax

In a Consultation Paper published in April 1991, the Government proposed a replacement for the community charge to come into effect from 1 April 1993 (non-domestic business rates will remain unchanged). Broadly this will reflect the capital value of properties, with reductions for single people, and those with second homes. If there are no concessions, the Church will be hard hit because parsonages will by and large fall in the higher capital value categories. Through the Churches Main Committee a response has been made to the Consultation Paper, requesting changes to reduce the estimated cost. At the time of writing, that response is awaited. Given the financial pressures which face the Church as a whole, it is very much hoped that concessions can be obtained.

Trust funds

The law relating to trust funds (investments) is very similar to that relating to trust property as already outlined. The managing trustees of any parish trusts ought to know the exact terms upon which the trust is held, under what conditions (if any) the capital may be touched, and for what purposes the interest may be applied. If this information is not in the terrier, it should be entered there when ascertained.

If money is invested in any holding from which tax is deducted at source, or where the dividend warrant includes an item marked 'tax credit', the tax should be reclaimed from the Inland Revenue Claims Branch if the trust is charitable. When the holding is in Government securities, it is possible to apply for the dividends to be paid gross. A form of application can be obtained from the Inland Revenue Claims Branch (see p. 119 below).

Title deeds, stock certificates etc.

It is obviously important that title deeds, stock certificates, and the like should be kept in a safe place. As to where that place should be, there is room for difference of opinion. It might be thought that the parish safe is the best place, but that is not necessarily so. Deeds get into wrong envelopes, or they find their way into the home of a parochial official who has a key to the safe and, with all the best will in the world, they sometimes get mislaid. Documents have in the past been discovered in the most unlikely places – they might be in the church safe, in the vicarage study, or in the churchwarden's attic. Sometimes it is hard not to use the term 'wilful neglect'.

Should they be kept in the bank, then? Yes, but some PCCs have a habit of changing their bank (often because there is a different bank nearer the home or work of the new treasurer) and if the 'safe custody' receipt is mislaid, or no one knows who holds it, then the documents may be so safe that no one can find them when they are needed.

Many Diocesan Boards of Finance will take parish deeds and certificates into safe keeping, and where there is this willingness, it should be taken advantage of. Where an investment or property is held on a trust which names the DBF as custodian trustee, then the deeds or certificates will be with the DBF, which usually has its own strong room.

If money is invested in any of the funds of the Central Board of Finance, there will be no certificates, because the CBF does not issue any. Stock certificates relating to investments in the name of the Official Custodian for Charities are held by the Bank of England, but deeds of property vested in the Official Custodian are not necessarily held in the Official Custodian's office. Again, the DBF may be willing to take them into its custody, and this is the best place.

Wherever the deeds or certificates are, the terrier should be kept in the church safe and there should be a note in it to say where the documents in question are lodged. Then there is no excuse for mislaying them.

What happens if a deed cannot be traced? If extensive enquiries fail to bring it to light, and if it is well known and without dispute that the PCC (or incumbent and wardens) have possession of the building in question, then a 'Statutory Declaration' can be made in support of the claim to ownership and in support of the known facts of a particular case. This procedure is not always acceptable to the purchaser or his solicitor, because there is always a residue of doubt, however small, that the title to the property has not been adequately demonstrated. Insurance can be taken out against this eventuality.

Finally ...

It will be clear from all this that a parish treasurer must alert his PCC to make adequate provision in its budget for the maintenance, insurance and repair of all properties for which it has responsibility.

Certain sums are known to be necessary every year: insurance premiums, parsonage water rate , parsonage repair assessment, a fifth of the fee for the architect to make his quinquennial inspection of the church building, where these are not integrated with the diocesan quota or share. The wise PCC will set aside a certain sum each year, over and above this, in (say) a 'Buildings Contingency Fund'. Then, when the quinquennial survey or report has revealed a number of urgent repairs, or when the church boiler breaks down, or the organ blower folds up, or the winter storms show up leaks in the roof, or new guttering is required on the curate's house, the parish will not be in blank despair with empty pockets, and there will be a basis on which to build up the funds needed. If the money is not needed for anything else, it can always be applied to the improvement of houses belonging to the PCC, because such improvements, besides making life easier for the present occupants, enhance the capital value of the asset if it is ever sold.

5

Insurances

There may be people around who believe that a Christian body ought not to include any item for insurances in its budget – did not Jesus tell us not to take care for the morrow, for the morrow will take care for itself? Many a parish treasurer has looked at the budget and the bills and been tempted to take the irresponsible way out. Unfortunately, it can't be done – not only are some insurances required by law, but incumbents, churchwardens and PCCs are trustees. As such it is their duty to take all necessary steps to ensure that the property with which they have been entrusted is properly maintained and handed on to the next generation. Insurance is a way of making sure that when disaster falls, it does not break the persons on whom it falls. It is, in fact, a very practical outworking of the Christian call to us to bear one another's burdens. The Church insurance policy money is not wasted if you make no claim on it that year; it helps people whose misfortune would have been too great for them to bear if they had had to carry it on their own.

Insurance is a technical matter, and this chapter will deal with the subject in a broad and simplified way. Detailed points should be taken up with the church's insurers, because there are generally special factors in individual cases.

Since most of the Anglican churches in England and Wales are insured with the Ecclesiastical Insurance Group, this chapter will be written from the point of view of the parish which has its cover with the EIG. Policies issued by other companies may not have identical details, but what we shall say below should still act as a broad guide even if your parish is one of the few which do not deal with the EIG.

The EIG is a specialist company, with wider knowledge of the intricacies of church insurance (and of the practicalities of parish finance) than any other. It offers policies specially designed for churches and other properties in ecclesiastical ownership. It is also – though this fact is not strictly relevant to the present chapter – a large general insurance office as well, dealing with commercial insurances in addition to personal covers such as motor, holiday and life schemes. Each year it ploughs back a substantial part of its profits into the Church, by way of grants. A significant part of these grants go to the diocesan boards of finance.

Review

Inflation makes it *essential* regularly to review the church's insurances. Despite repeated and frequent pleas, there are still many parishes which are seriously under-insured because of rising prices. In such cases, if there were to be a serious fire, the PCC would be in a most embarrassing position. There could even be cases in which individual members of a PCC could be held responsible at law, out of their own personal estate, to the maximum amount they possessed, for claims made on them by third parties. This is because, under the law of tort, if a member of a PCC is aware of the dangerous condition of a church building and takes no steps to prevent injury to third parties, he could be held liable in the tort of negligence.

Even if at first glance the losses (after a fire or a burglary, for instance) were less than the amount for which the building was insured, it could be that only a fraction of the loss would be repaid. This is because of the application of what is known as the principle of average. An 'average' clause appears on nearly all fire insurance policies, and has the effect of relating the payment available for any loss to the adequacy of the sum insured. If the sum insured is (at the time of the loss) less than the value of the property to which it relates, then the payment is scaled down in the proportion that the sum insured bears to the actual value. For example:

Value of the property at time of fire	£1,000,000
Sum insured	£600,000
Amount of loss	£100,000

Although the loss is much less than the sum insured, it will not be paid in full. The sum insured is only six-tenths of the value of the property, and the church will receive only £60,000 towards making good £100,000 worth of damage.

For insurance effected with the EIG, as a concession in the case of church insurance, 'average' will not apply if the sum insured is at least 75 per cent of the amount properly insurable. Thus in the example above, 'average' would apply; but if the church had been insured for £750,000 or more, the condition would not have operated and the whole of the loss would have been repaid.

This is an important principle of which the church treasurer must be aware. It means that if the amount insured has been allowed to fall behind the true value insurable, the church is at real risk – and since most fires are partial rather than total, the under-insured PCC will be left with an expensive repair programme and insufficient funds. The churchwardens and treasurer should therefore make it a matter of priority to find out *for themselves* when the insurance figures were last revised and whether the present figures are adequate. It is not good enough to assume that someone else will do this. That is a sure recipe for letting the matter go by default.

Nowadays, many insurance policies have a built-in index-linked clause to allow for inflation. If there is no such clause in your policy, it is your duty to review the amount annually. Even if there is such a clause, the cover ought to be reviewed at three-year intervals to make sure that the amounts are not getting out of line with building and repair costs.

The EIG will be ready to offer advice. Remember, however, that the responsibility for the final decision with regard to the amount of cover to be obtained rests with the PCC.

Church buildings – structure and contents

Many church buildings are, by their nature, irreplaceable. They may be of great importance from an historical or architectural point of view. They may contain beautifully-carved woodwork, ancient plate or even ancient books and vestments. It is clear that a full reinstatement or replacement as existing would not be possible in such cases. When assessing an amount on which to base the fire insurance figure, work on a sum which will be adequate to meet the cost of a proper scheme of restoration (including architects' and other professional fees and VAT). It would not be usual to aim at the full and absolute cost of reinstatement of all the treasures of the building. What needs to be borne in mind is the extent to which a church might be damaged before it could be regarded as, constructionally, a total loss, at which point a more simple modern building might be acceptable as a replacement.

The basic EIG options for insurance against fire, lightning, and explosion are:

(a) Orthodox basis

In normal situations this is the scheme to aim at. In arriving at cover on this basis it would be assumed that in the event of partial loss, repair in similar form would be required, but that at a certain point the structure would be regarded as a total loss and rebuilding would be undertaken using modern techniques and materials to provide comparable facilities on the most economic terms. The figures sub-mitted for the guidance of parishes following a visit by an EIG surveyor can (see p. 49) above) be reduced to 75 per cent without invoking the 'average' penalty for under-insurance. It is essential to remember, however, that an insurance arranged on this basis must be revised each year to reflect inflation.

(b) Nominal first loss

This type of policy is free of 'average'. The sum insured is on a limited basis, not usually exceeding 20 per cent of the figure for which one might insure under the orthodox basis. It will provide for a modest scheme of repairs or, in the event of more serious damage, the cost of demolition and/or making safe, and a small sum will be left over as the nucleus of a fund for some alternative project. This type of policy may be suitable if the future of the church building is in doubt. It provides very limited cover at low cost. It is essential to consult with your rural dean or archdeacon before agreeing to accept the risk that the building would not be replaced in the case of severe damage.

(c) Negotiable basis

As a specialist company, the EIG is ready to negotiate individually with any parish where the options under (a) and (b) above are not thought suitable. Experience has shown that there are parishes where cover beyond the limits of (b) is required but nevertheless orthodox insurance is seen as inappropriate. Each case is discussed with the parish and looked at on its individual merits so that some-thing can be tailored to meet the particular situation.

Policies under (a), (b) and (c) above are always index-linked.

Basic risks are against fire, lightning, and explosion. In addition, cover may be secured against all or any of the following optional extensions, and it is for the parish and company to agree which of these is appropriate and worth covering:

   (i) storm or tempest,
  (ii) flood,
 (iii) bursting or overflowing of water tanks, apparatus or pipes,
 (iv) impact by road vehicles, horses or cattle,
  (v) aircraft and other aerial devices or articles dropped therefrom,
 (vi) riot and civil commotion,
(vii) malicious damage (this can only be insured in conjunction with (vi) above,
(viii) earthquake.

In addition to the insurance of the fabric of the church building, there will need to be insurance of the contents. 'All risks' and theft cover should be taken out to provide insurance for the church plate, altar furnishings and the organ against loss or damage due to any accident or misfortune. This will not include gradual deterioration, wear and tear, damp, mildew, rust, dust, vermin, mechanical or electrical derangement or breakdown, or loss or damage due to any process of cleaning, restoration or repair. Special cover is available for organ parts when dismantled.

If the church contains any special treasures (such as Elizabethan chalices or an ancient library) special cover should be arranged. If such treasures are, in effect, irreplaceable because of their rarity or antiquity, it may be in order to insure them, not for their real value, which may run into tens of thousands of pounds, but for the cost of a 'good modern replacement'. If it is decided not to insure ancient libraries at their true replacement value, it is well at least to insure for the cost of repair. There could be a fire which caused less than total loss, and fire hoses could do very expensive damage to ancient leather bindings, the repair of which is a time-consuming and expert business.

The general furniture and fittings should be insured against theft. This includes cover against damage to the building caused in an attempt to steal the contents. Provision is also possible (and desirable) to cover theft of clothing and personal effects of clergy, choir, and officials whilst on the premises. Lead on the roof and elsewhere is at great risk, as (to a lesser extent) are other metallic roof coverings. An item can be included for this, but the premium is very high because there have been so many thefts in recent years. If you want to have your lead covered against theft, negotiate this specially. You may find it particularly difficult to get cover for second or subsequent thefts within a stated period. The crime prevention officer at your local police station may have advice to offer, as may specialist firms concerned with security, but only approach well-known and reliably recommended organizations. It may be possible (and certainly cheaper) to get faculty approval for the replacement of lead by shorter-lasting but less theft-prone coverings.

Cover is also available against theft of money. The sum insured should be the maximum expected to be at risk at any one time. Cash should be recorded as soon as possible after being received, entered in the services register book, and placed immediately in the church safe until such time as it can be taken to the bank. If, then, there were to be a theft, exact information can be given to the police and insurance company. Alms boxes and other containers for money should be emptied as frequently as possible (and the fact that this is done should be stated nearby). Cover extends until the cash has been banked. The insurance does not cover losses due to mismanagement by church officials, though the insurance can be extended to cover losses due to misappropriation by those handling the cash on behalf of the PCC. Fortunately, losses from this cause are rare.

Finally, the church policy may be extended to cover the breakage of fixed glass and sanitary fittings. This should relate to all glass – stained and otherwise. The premium is modest, as it supplements the perils covered by extension of the fire policy.

Normally, insurance cover for a church relates only to a church building in use for worship. If the building ceases to be so used (whether permanently by reason of a declaration of redundancy or temporarily because of works being carried out to the building) special considerations apply, and the insurance company must be notified immediately.

Public liability (third party) insurance

Whatever decisions are made about fire insurance and other risks, there should always be proper legal liability insurance for an adequate amount. This is because in the case of accidents to members of the public, the courts may award substantial damages. A public liability insurance making provision for protection up to at least £1,000,000 in respect of any one accident is essential. The EIG policy extends to protect the interests of the church authorities in respect of legal liability for accidents or damage elsewhere in the United Kingdom in connection with any church function, fete, or other parochial activity.

It is an essential condition of any public liability insurance that the property being insured is maintained in good order.

Employers' liability insurance

This form of insurance is compulsory under the terms of the Employers' Liability (Compulsory Insurance) Act 1969. It protects church authorities against claims for damages made by paid church employees who have sustained injury while carrying out their church duties. A certificate to the effect that cover has been procured has to be displayed by the church.

Group personal accident insurance

This policy (normal age limits 11–75 years) is designed to alleviate hardship to those injured in the service of the church by providing stated monetary benefits. These are payable irrespective of any question of legal liability on the part of the church authorities to make any payment. Groups which may be covered are:

(a) the parochial clergy;
(b) paid employees (other than assistant clergy and bellringers);
(c) bellringers;
(d) unpaid churchworkers;
(e) church officers (assault cover).

Benefits are either weekly payments (up to a maximum of 104 weeks) during temporary total disablement, or a single lump sum payable in the event of death, loss of one or more limbs or eyes, or total and permanent disablement.

The clergy are covered for the full 24 hours, but employees are only covered whilst carrying out their paid duties, and volunteer churchworkers are covered whilst carrying out their unpaid work in the premises insured by the policy.

Church halls

The EIG 'Hall Combined' insurance covers the main risks of fire, lightning and explosion (with the optional extensions), public and employers' liability insurance, theft and breakage of fixed glass and sanitary fixtures. As the basic information regarding these items is substantially the same as for the insurance of the church building, it is not repeated here. There are a few additional points, however, which relate more to a hall than a church.

Some halls are quite extensive and may have camping equipment, musical instruments (such as bugles and drums used by the Church Lads' and Church Girls' Brigade), record players, music centres etc. stored within them. The PCC must be quite clear (and must make it clear to these other users) who is responsible for the insurance of such contents. The CLCGB may have its own insurance, in which case the PCC will not be involved. If the camping equipment belongs to an organization such as the Scouts or Guides, enquiries should be made to ensure that the organization has its own insurance protection. If the PCC is to be responsible, the insurance company must be informed.

If a member of a group or organization brings musical instruments, record players, or hi-fi equipment into the hall and leaves them there, he must be told (preferably in writing) that they should be covered by his own insurance and that the PCC cannot accept responsibility.

If a hall is used by a playgroup, the organizers should have their own liability insurance. They may also have their equipment insured. It would be wise to make sure of the facts and not make any assumptions which could prove to be ill-founded. When the time comes to make a claim, it is far too late to discover that each organization thought the other was providing cover.

The church complex

If a church and/or a hall and/or a house or flat form a 'complex' of buildings it is wise to have the whole complex under a single policy (unless one part of the complex is a parsonage house, for which see below). If there is a church, hall, and residence, the policy can be the EIG 'Church Combined' policy. If it is a hall and house or flat, it will be the 'Hall Combined' policy, it being made clear in the policy that part of the hall structure has a residential use.

The parsonage house

Section 12 of the Repair of Benefice Buildings Measure 1972 makes Diocesan Parsonages Boards responsible for insuring 'all the parsonage houses in their diocese against all such risks as are included in the usual form of houseowner's policy relating to buildings' (see also pp. 14–15 and 38). The policies are comprehensive and claims should be made via the Diocesan Parsonages Board (or Parsonages Committee if the DBF is the Parsonages Board and has delegated its functions). This policy covers the building only. The contents of the parsonage house are the occupant's responsibility and it is for him to insure them separately if he wishes them to be covered. The PCC treasurer may wish to discuss this with the incumbent.

Other houses

If the parish owns other houses – for full-time or part-time curate, deacon, lay worker, verger, or caretaker – it should cover them by a house-owner's comprehensive policy. The EIG policy includes

(a) Fire, explosion, lightning, earthquake; storm, tempest, flood, subsidence or landslip; riot and malicious damage; aircraft; bursting or overflowing of water tanks, pipes, or apparatus; theft; impact by vehicles; leakage of oil from fixed oil-fired heating installations; breaking or collapse of television or radio aerials.
(b) Breakage of fixed glass and sanitary ware.
(c) Accidental damage to underground pipes, electricity and telephone cables.

(d) Legal liability to pay damages and costs for accidents to third parties.

(e) Loss of rent.

Details of comprehensive policies vary greatly and the prospectus or policy should be studied for the finer details.

The policy issued by the EIG is automatically index-linked, using the House Rebuilding Cost Index issued by the British Insurance Association. The amount covered is adjusted monthly in line with the index, and no charge is made for any increase in cover during the period of insurance. Normally, 'average' does not apply, but the attention of PCCs is drawn to the declaration which has to be signed by the proposer, which (*inter alia*) states that the 'amount to be insured on the buildings as described represents not less than the full rebuilding value'. The rebuilding value is, of course, usually a quite different figure from the amount which might be obtained from a sale on the open market.

Other liabilities

Care should be taken not to overlook including in the public liability policy any buildings occupied for church purposes even though they may not be owned by the Church. This is referred to as 'occupiers' liability risk'. It is also necessary to maintain public liability insurance on a building owned by the church and leased or rented out. A property-owner may be liable for accidents in such premises.

Security

Vandalism and an increased number of thefts create great security difficulties. Many parishes have had to decide to keep their churches locked except when services are being held. Others, however, prefer to lock up the more valuable items, to enable a church to be kept open for prayer and for visitors. But oversight is important – apart from thefts and general vandalism, many major fires have followed casual entry through open doors. Incumbents, churchwardens and PCCs must take all reasonable precautions to protect the church and its contents from these risks. In particular:

Money should be locked in a safe. Alms boxes or wall safes should be emptied frequently, and the money banked as soon as possible (see pp. 52–3).

It is a wise precaution to have items of value photographed (and copies of the photographs should be kept in places other than the church) to help in the recovery of stolen items.

Fire extinguishers should be provided in prominent positions in all buildings to which the public has access. The number depends upon the size and geography of the building, but the organ and the boiler house are two obviously essential places.

Electrical and heating systems, and lightning conductors, need to be regularly checked – at least at every quinquennial inspection.

The EIG has issued a series of technical advice sheets on these and other matters, which are obtainable on application.

6

Giving to God – and getting it back from Caesar

So far, we have written almost entirely about what goes *out* of the parish accounts. What about the parish's income? In most parish accounts, the largest items of income will appear under some such headings as 'collections' or 'envelopes' or 'pledged giving', and 'reclaimed tax'. A great deal lies behind those simple headings.

'The collection' does not mean simply the result of passing a plate round the congregation during service-time, in the expectation that people will dip quickly, without much thought, into purse or pocket and fetch out a 50p piece. In a Christian context, a 'collection' needs to represent something that is carefully thought out, the reason for which lies in the very nature of God giving himself and of his relation to us.

Let us, then, go back to first principles. The place to begin when we think of Christian stewardship is the very first chapters of the Bible. The world in which we live, our very being, is God-given. We neither asked for it nor earned it. God is the creator, man is in his image (Gen 1.27) and God has 'breathed life-giving breath into his nostrils' (Gen 2.7). Until God breathed the breath of life into him, man was useless. (There is a parallel in the New Testament, in John 20. The disciples after the crucifixion were powerless until the risen Jesus came and breathed on them and said, 'Receive the Holy Spirit'.)

When we give something away, it is no longer under our control, but under the control of the person to whom we have given it. He may use it in a way of which we could approve; but he is free to do otherwise. So with the life, the being, which God gave us. It is ours and we can do what we like with it. The tragedy in the world is that the great majority of mankind forgets (or does not realize) that God has given them all they have and all they are – so they do what they will with their lives in disregard of God. Because of man's heedless rebellion, God had to enter an even more costly act of giving; this time, of self-giving, even to the death on the Cross.

God's giving, then, has two dimensions. First he gave us ourselves, then he gave us himself. Christians are people who have realized this. On them has dawned the realization of something of the depth and the breadth and the height of the self-giving love of God and so they determine to respond to God in a similar way – by giving back to God the life that God has given to them.

The love of God was total. No less total a love is demanded of Christians. Love cannot calculate parts and bits; love involves the whole of a person or it is not true love. Our response to the love of God is a response which gives back our whole being to its source, dedicated to his service, allowing him to transform us, and putting aside worldly standards. We then know that we do not belong to ourselves but to God, who bought us at a price; so we use our bodies to God's glory (see 1 Cor 6.19, 20). When we give ourselves to Christ there is a new creation. The old has gone, the new is come. Christians live a style of life which is radically different from that of non-Christians. God comes first, in their choice of a job, in their use of time, in their application of their talents – and in the disposition of their wealth. Money is no more than one aspect of the life of total Christian stewardship.

'Stewardship' is an idea which has been heard in Church circles a lot of late. A steward is a person who looks after the belongings or the estate of another, and it is his duty to care diligently for his master's property. Paul writes to Titus (1.7) that a Christian leader must be of unimpeachable character because he is God's steward, caring for the Church on God's behalf. In 1 Corinthians 4, the ministers of Christ are termed stewards of the mysteries of God, and bidden to be faithful. 1 Peter 4.10 bids all God's people to be stewards of the manifold gifts of his grace, using these gifts in the service of one another to God's glory. To use the word 'stewardship' acknowledges that all we have, we have as a trust from God and that we must therefore look after all our possessions to God's glory. God has put into our hands a certain amount of money, and the way we dispose of it will mirror our understanding of our responsibility to serve him and his kingdom. Some of that money is necessarily used up in the discharge of our family duties and civic responsibilities – homes, food, clothing and taxes. Some of that money is rightly used up for our own entertainment and pleasure. But unless *all* of that money is used in the knowledge that we belong to God and that he has first claim on our lives, then we are not spending *any* of it as Christians. Otherwise, 'the collection' will simply represent the odd change left over when everything else has been provided for, and our Christian lives will be the same – God and his kingdom will be a spare-time activity fitted into the times when there is nothing better to do. The money we give, and the way we decide about how to give it, are surefire indications of the place God has in the whole of our life. And that goes, not only for our personal budget, but for the PCC budget as well – giving to God needs to be accorded a priority over domestic spending, or it may be squeezed out altogether (see, further, pp. 87–9 below).

Stewardship, then, is 'not so much "the collection", more a way of life'. It does not come easily or naturally to most people or to most PCCs. It has to be taught, discussed, and fully understood if it is to be effective. It is not an optional extra which can be grafted on to a Church which is lacking in zeal, fellowship, and an understanding of the implications of the Gospel. The treasurer who looks at the church books, finds that they don't balance, and suggests that 'what we need to get us out of the red is a stewardship campaign', knows nothing of the costingness and life-changing nature of what is entailed in taking stewardship seriously. Nor does the parson who thinks stewardship is the quick answer to the financial problems, associated with a leaking roof or a broken-down organ. (It is the answer, but it is not quick – it needs to be tackled at the level of broken-down fellowship and leaking discipleship before a word can be said about roof or organ.) Stewardship can be taught in a church which is beginning to respond to biblical goals and is open to change. If the church fellowship has no clear goals, responds only to crises, and is resistant to change, then teaching about stewardship will have to begin a great deal further back. It will involve, often, years of pre-planning and basic teaching about the Gospel and our response to the Gospel. If we try to slap on stewardship like slapping a plaster on a deep wound without treating the underlying malady, we shall end up worse than we started – with a disillusioned congregation which thinks it has tried stewardship and that 'it doesn't work in a place like this', when in fact it has not even begun to cotton on to what the whole thing is about. Stewardship is the practical application of the biblical teaching about commitment of life in response to the outgoing love of God. Unless it is seen in these terms, it will deserve the failure that will come.

Just as 'we love, because he first loved us', so we give because he first gave to us. And the motive of our giving is love. That will mean that giving goes high on our list of priorities, and will absorb a significant percentage of our income – both our personal income and also the income of our PCC. That 'significant percentage' in Old Testament times was the tithe or tenth (Gen 28.22), and what was offered to God was not the last bit left over, but the first-fruits (Deut 26.10). Yet, miraculously and paradoxically, the men of the Old Testament found that if they gave to God first, without caring for their own well-being or prosperity, God would bless them more richly than they had given to him. We too will find the same if we make it a budget priority to give a good slice of our income for God's purposes. 'Some people', said the writer of Proverbs (11.24–25), 'spend their money freely and still grow richer. Others are cautious and yet grow poorer. Be generous, and you will be prosperous. Help others, and you will be helped.' The same teaching was echoed by Jesus when he told his followers that if they were 'concerned above everything else with the kingdom of God and what he requires' then he would provide them with all those other things (Matt 6.33). God's promises to those who give are fantastic – 'Give to others, and God will give to you. Indeed you will receive a full measure, a generous helping, poured into your hands – all that you can hold. The measure you use for others is the one that God will use for you' (Luke 6.38). St Paul followed this teaching up when he wrote that 'the person who sows few seeds will have a small crop, the one who sows many seeds will have a large crop, Each one should give, then, as he has decided, not with regret or out of a sense of duty; for God loves the one who gives gladly' (2 Cor 9.6–7). The whole of chapters 8 and 9 of 2 Corinthians is well worth reading in this context, especially in a modern version. Paul is holding up the Macedonians as examples – they were generous because (8.5) 'first they gave *themselves* unto the Lord'. When people are converted, and when they realize that Jesus is their Lord and Saviour, they *give* – not 'with regret or (merely) out of a sense of duty' but deep, loving giving out of deep gratitude for God's unfailing love. The Greek behind that word 'gladly' in 2 Corinthians 9.7 (in some translations, 'God loves a cheerful giver') is 'hilarious'. Are we hilarious, cheerful, glad to give? If we are, we know why; it is because (2 Cor 9.15) we are, in that way, thanking God for his gift which is beyond words.

> When I survey the wondrous Cross
>   On which the Prince of Glory died,
> My richest gain I count but loss,
>   And pour contempt on all my pride.
>
> Were the whole realm of nature mine,
>   That were an offering far too small;
> Love so amazing, so divine,
>   Demands my soul, my life, my all.

We make no apology for this exposition of the theology of steward-ship within a handbook of parish finance. Parish finance is Christian finance, and if money is not handled sacramentally by Christians, they are keeping God at arm's length in a matter which is of close

and intimate concern to them. If, on the other hand, they can be
open to God in this aspect of their life, then the barriers between
God and them will have been breached in a deeply significant way,
and the whole character of their Christian life will be transformed.
The whole flavour of 'parish finance' in a parish which has taken the
underlying concepts of stewardship on board is so different as to defy
description. The only way to be convinced is to try it out!

When we come down to the detailed answer to the question, 'How
much, then, shall I give?', it must immediately be recognized that
there is no hard-and-fast rule. 'Circumstances alter cases.' Very
many Christians, in all walks of life, do 'tithe' in the Old Testament
meaning of the word. They give one-tenth of their income to the
Church, and they find that they still have plenty left to lead a
normal, happy, and fulfilled life. Some give 'love offerings' over their
tithe.

Others may feel that this is too big a step from their present level
of giving and will opt for a lesser percentage – 8 or 5 per cent, say.
What is important is that the level of giving should be decided after
prayer and as a matter of personal conscience and commitment.
Some may wish to express their tithing as a percentage of gross pay,
others as a proportion related to their 'take-home' pay after tax and
National Insurance deductions have been made. The chart printed
in Appendix 1 (p. 99) is a useful way of working out one's percentage
giving at various levels of weekly income.

In making a decision, it might be good to set down one's personal
income and anticipated expenditure. At the top of the list of expenditure will have to come the unavoidables – tax, National Insurance
deductions, Union levies, etc.; rent or mortgage repayments. Giving
back to God should head this list, and not be with the 'extras' at the
bottom. When the right amount has been decided, it then needs to
be divided into that proportion which goes to the Church and that
proportion which is available for donations to other charities, special
appeals, etc.

If there is to be a decision to have a stewardship campaign or
stewardship mission in a parish (and the latter term is to be pre-
ferred, as it conjures up the idea of a wider commitment of one's self,
whereas 'campaign' is redolent of a solely money-raising effort),
then it is essential that the incumbent and the PCC treasurer
initially, and the whole of the PCC eventually, should have a proper
grasp of the principles of stewardship, and they should have first
applied them in their own lives before they dare to commend them
to others. As was said of Chaucer's Parson.

> But Christ's lore, and his apostles twelve,
> He taught, but first he followed it himself.

It all boils down to being able to accept the saying, 'freely you have received; freely give'.

Stewardship missions

No book can give a complete guide to conducting a stewardship campaign or stewardship mission, because each parish is unique. There is no substitute for seeking out others who have done it before and having long and detailed discussion with them to see what a mission might involve. Friends in neighbouring parishes who have gone through it all recently can give some idea of the likely scale of the operation and can help you to answer such questions as whether you have the lay potential, and what kinds of help and on what scale you will need them. Candid friends who know the parish (the rural dean? the archdeacon?) can help assess whether the parish is ready to accept the teaching which will be necessary as a ground-basis for a successful stewardship mission, or whether the ground needs to be prepared over a longer period and at a deeper level. Many dioceses employ a full-time stewardship Adviser or Stewardship Director, and he should be brought into the discussions at an early stage.

Basically there are four ways of mounting a parish stewardship mission:

1 The mission can be directed by the diocesan stewardship adviser/ organizer or members of his team. Dioceses differ about the charging of fees, but it is not usually at a commercial rate.
2 A team may come in from another parish which has had missions itself and has accumulated enough knowledge and expertise to help others.
3 It is possible to employ a professional fund-raising organization. A commercial fee will be charged, and it may well seem heavy. Some organizations charge fees 'on results' but most will require a fairly substantial 'priming of the pump' and will have a basic component of the charge which is payable whatever the results of the campaign.
4 Some parishes opt for an entirely 'do-it-yourself' scheme. This is not to be recommended. A deal of professional expertise is necessary; the campaign director ought to have few (if any) other commitments for the period of the campaign and for some time before and afterwards. It is easier for someone from outside to be 'tough' with the parish and with local helpers; and if tensions have arisen, they can more easily be borne by someone who does not have to live afterwards with the people amongst whom they have been generated. In all but a few cases, the results of 'do-it-your-

self' campaigns are meagre and disappointing compared with the potential of the other three methods.

Every stewardship mission needs a missioner, director, organizer, or adviser (by whatever name he is known) who is in ultimate charge, and who will work primarily through a co-ordinating committee. The incumbent should not be the missioner; he has other wider functions. The missioner and the committee will work out such details as the scale of the campaign, how many families are to be approached, how the list of families is to be arrived at, what the goals and targets are, how the necessary teaching is to be got across, what the programme is, how long needs to be allocated to each phase of the operation, and so on.

The missioner and the parish committee will need to agree on the nature and scope of the preparatory work, the recruitment of the visiting team and its training, and the method by which the mission is 'launched' when the time comes. Some parishes believe that a full-scale 'loyalty dinner' is necessary to explain the working of the mission; others believe it is better to do things less lavishly. There will need to be literature explaining the mission and commending it to the parishioners. Often the diocesan bishop is asked to contribute a message. Any printed matter needs to be expertly laid-out on the page as well as being carefully prepared and well written. Printing, design, and typography are all important. Anything too lavish might suggest that the parish has no need of extra funds; anything unprofessional and slapdash suggests that 'anything goes' and invites a less than whole-hearted response. The mission must be directed at the committed members of the Church, in order to motivate them to make their giving match their Christian commitment. The emphasis must not be on the need of the Church to receive funds, but on the need for Christians to make a more realistic response to God's giving. We are not after charity but commitment. This does not mean that financial goals do not need to be set, or that the financial needs of the Church ought not to be precisely given. They should; but they should not be seen to be determinative of the whole operation.

Already we can see some of the areas in which there will need to be careful organization. The co-ordinating committee should be aware of all these, but should be ready to delegate the actual working-out of these to *ad hoc* groups. It is most important that everyone who is approached with a view to declaring his 'pledge' or 'promise' should be approached personally. A letter (even a letter with an enclosed form and a reply-paid envelope) is no good. People have to be visited, in their own homes, by people who have themselves accepted the principles of Christian stewardship, so that they may themselves decide on their personal response. This visiting will not be done by the campaign director, but by a team of visitors whom he has trained.

The choosing, persuading, and training of this visiting team is probably the most important single aspect of the mission. Of course people will feel frightened at the thought of doing this. Of course they will feel shy. They will probably feel embarrassed at the thought of talking to other people about two such personal subjects as God and money. They will feel inadequate, and will imagine that they could never answer all the questions that they expect to be asked. All this is natural, and to be expected. The campaign director knows it. He knows that it is his business to train, instruct, and guide the team both beforehand and as they are going through their programme of visits. He will give a great deal of his time to this, which will have a high priority within his conduct of the mission. And the campaign director is not the only source of help. The visitors should never forget, even when they are trembling on someone's doorstep, that they are doing God's work. God will grant power and strength, and will give them the words to say if they have done their own work of preparation as well as they can.

Those who are visited will be asked to think about, and pray over, their response. They will probably be given a pledge card on which they will fill in the amount they promise to give weekly towards God's work in the parish. This is a promise, not a legally-binding document. If the person wants to vary the amount (either because his circumstances have changed or because he finds he has promised too much or too little) he can do so, but he ought then to inform the recorder (see p. 66). The total on the cards will enable the PCC to prepare a budget more accurately for the normal work of the parish and missionary giving, as well as to plan for a major project if this was included in the 'aims' of the campaign. Those who pledge should also be asked to enter into a deed of covenant (about which more will be said later in this chapter) so that the parish may have the benefit of reclaimable tax.

In many stewardship missions, the pledge cards will also enable people to volunteer their help for the work of the parish in any one of a number of ways in which their time and their talents can be put to use in God's service.

During the course of the campaign numbered envelopes will have been purchased into which people may put their (weekly or monthly) pledged amounts and bring them to church. There may well be an occasion at the end of the visiting period of the mission at which the pledge cards are offered formally, and the congregation pray for God's grace to help them keep the promises they have made and to help them live the committed Christian lives to which these pledges bear witness.

Thereafter, each week, returned envelopes will be opened and the amount in each envelope will be recorded. There needs to be a recorder (preferably – to spread the load – someone other than the PCC treasurer). It is most important that the donors should be assured of complete confidentiality, so the persons who administer the contributions should be known to be persons of discretion. It is quite easy to ensure that when the envelopes are opened and their contents recorded, confidentiality is observed as to who makes what contribution. The envelopes will have simply a number and a date on them, and they can be recorded in the book by number. The key with the names and addresses corresponding to the numbers should be quite separate from the book; if it is thought either necessary or desirable, it can be kept by a different person, and the key and record book need never be brought together (see also p. 79 below).

The stewardship mission should never be the end of the matter. It is essential to have a continuation committee whose task it will be to carry on the educative process begun at the mission, to help those who want further information, and to see that when new people join the worshipping community, they are invited to join the stewardship scheme. Enthusiasm is rarely self-generating and it is wise to have periodical renewal campaigns – not (usually) every year but certainly every three or four years at least. It is a good idea, however, to have a 'stewardship Sunday' annually just before new envelopes are distributed, as this helps to remind people of the need to review and revise their giving each year. The renewal campaign will not be as large-scale an operation as the original one; but it will enable members to revise their giving in the light of their changed circumstances and of alterations in their wages and salaries. Wherever possible contributors should be urged to revise their amounts every time their income changes – which in many cases will be annually.

Pledges and covenants

A pledge and a covenant are not the same. A *pledge* is a promise made to the parish, which should represent a carefully and prayerfully worked-out 'tithe' given to God for his work in the parish and elsewhere. The fact that a promise has been made and a dated series of envelopes given in which the promised money can be placed, helps to focus the mind on the need for regular giving – even if the worshipper is sometimes away from church on a particular Sunday.

A *covenant* is an undertaking made under a legal deed – usually in such circumstances as will enable the recipient to recover the tax which the donor has paid on the amount given. Under present UK law, if a person who pays tax at basic rate on any part of his income covenants to give to a charity over a period capable of exceeding three years, that charity can reclaim the tax which has been paid on the gift. So (if the basic rate of income tax stands at 25 per cent) a person who earns £1.34 pays 34p in tax and keeps the £1 for himself. If he gives this £1 to charity under a deed of covenant, that charity can reclaim the 34p from the Inland Revenue, and this has been done at no extra cost to the donor.

Since 6 April 1990 husbands and wives have been treated as wholly independent for tax purposes. This means that each of them is taxed separately on his or her own income instead of being assessed jointly for tax. Fuller details of the change are contained in the leaflet IR 80 which you can get from any tax office or tax enquiry centre.

One important consequence of this change is that each of them is also treated separately when they covenant. For example, in the past if the wife was making payments under a covenant made by her alone but had no income of her own, the tax she deducted was treated as satisfied out of the tax paid on her husband's income. But with Independent Taxation this is no longer possible. If she is not already paying tax on income of her own, she should pay the tax deducted to the Inland Revenue; for her, therefore, there will be no tax advantage in giving by way of covenant. A married couple likely to be in this position may find it worthwhile to consider changing their arrangements.

Sometimes a covenant is made *jointly* by a husband and wife. When that happens, both of them are jointly liable to make the payments due under the covenant. If there is no agreement to the contrary, they should pay an equal share of the amount covenanted; and each of them is entitled to claim tax relief on the amount he or she pays. But if the couple agree that the *taxpaying* spouse will make the whole payment, he or she will be entitled to the full relief.

The covenant as a way of increasing parochial income is exploited by far too few churches, and the next section will deal with the practicalities and queries to which the law of covenants gives rise. Deeds of covenant are not liable to stamp duty.

Deeds of covenant

In order for tax to be reclaimed, a deed of covenant must be made between a donor and a charity. A PCC is a charity and does not need to be specifically registered as such. The deed must be in such a form as enables it to run for a period which exceeds three years. In practice, most covenants will be made for four years at a time, after which a new deed will have to be signed. All covenants are cancelled by death and do not form a charge on the estate of a covenantor who dies during the currency of the covenant. The amount covenanted can be expressed as an annual sum, or as a quarterly, monthly or weekly one. A person who puts 10p a week in the church collection can make a covenant for that amount. It is hoped that the covenanted sum will not be as small as that, but the example is given to show that nobody need feel frightened of the idea of covenanting. For tax to be reclaimed by the PCC, tax must have been paid by the donor. Recorders must ensure that the full amount of the covenant has been received.

There are still many people who hesitate before committing themselves to a covenant. Four years may sound a long time. What happens if they are unable to continue the payments? Can they be compelled to continue if they find themselves (for instance) out of a job before the covenant has finished? What about the tax reclaimed if the covenant is not completed? Is the donor responsible then for repaying it? These fears should not be allowed to stop people covenanting. The covenant is made with the PCC, *not* with the Inland Revenue. If the covenantor defaults, the only body which can take any action to enforce the covenant is the PCC, and it is hardly likely to do this. The Inland Revenue is powerless to enforce a covenant, and it is not a party to it. If payments lapse, the Inland Revenue cannot reclaim any money which it has already paid over to the PCC by reason of that covenant, though – of course – neither can the PCC continue to reclaim tax in subsequent years.

In the past the Inland Revenue accepted deeds of covenant in which there was an 'escape clause' to the effect that payments under the deed would cease if certain contingencies arose. The Inland Revenue has now received legal advice that many such 'escape clauses' invalidate the covenant for tax purposes, because their effect can be that the covenantor can of his own volition terminate it without the consent of the charity concerned. Some deeds of covenant which have in the past been accepted by the Inland Revenue as valid, and on which repayment of tax has already been made, are, in fact, invalid. They will, however, continue to be treated as effective for tax purposes until they expire and, provided payments are made, tax refunds to charities will not be refused.

What happens if a person, having decided on his 'tithe', receives an increase in wages or salary and wants to increase his covenanted amount? All that is necessary is to complete and sign a superseding deed of covenant. This will replace the original deed, and the new deed will run for four years from the new date. An alternative would be to enter into new deeds for additional contributions, but this makes for complications in that the different deeds will then have different expiry dates.

The deed of covenant must be signed and dated by the donor in the presence of an independent witness, who must also sign, and any alterations should be initialled. The date of the first payment *must be on or after the date of the deed.* The Inland Revenue has, in the past, accepted retrospective covenants – e.g. a covenantor could sign a deed at some time during the year (say October) covering payments made earlier in the tax year, but a court case has made it clear that this practice does not conform to the law. The practice is of long standing and so, in order to allow charities to bring their practices into line without hardship, the Inland Revenue will, where claims have previously been made on this basis, continue to accept such claims, for covenants made before 31 July 1990. The Inland Revenue has issued guidance aimed at simplifying the making of a covenant to assist charities and individuals to ensure that their covenants are legally effective. A deed of covenant in the form set out on pp. 102–3 is acceptable to the Inland Revenue for covenants made after 31 July 1990.

PCCs may copy their own deeds of covenant provided they are in the form as set out on pp. 102–3 (any variations should be agreed with the Inland Revenue), or copies may be obtained from the diocesan stewardship office or the Central Board of Finance. The words 'Deed of Covenant' must be printed at the top of the form, but the requirement that the deed had to be executed under seal has been abolished. The specimen deed is a net deed, and specifies the amount to be paid by the donor to the PCC, out of his taxed income. If there is a variation in the rate of income tax, it is the PCC which gains or loses – the donor pays the same amount. Thus, if the deed is for £1, the PCC reclaims 34p if the basic rate of tax is 25 per cent. If (which God forbid!) the basic rate of tax were to rise to 50 per cent, the donor would still pay his £1, but as he would have had to earn £2 and pay £1 tax in order to have that £1 in his pocket, the PCC could then reclaim £1 instead of 34p.

There is an additional advantage if the donor pays tax at above the basic rate. Legislation provides that those who pay tax at higher rates may claim tax relief on their covenanted payments *at higher rates*, subject to a ceiling of relief on £3,000 p.a. Their covenant will therefore cost them less and they could be persuaded to increase the amount for which they covenant. For example: if a donor is paying tax at 40p in the pound on the top slice of his income, let us suppose he wishes his gift to the PCC to cost him £120 a year. He should covenant for £150. The PCC will receive this £150 from him plus a further £50 in tax reclaimed by the PCC (being the basic rate of tax at 25 per cent on £200 – i.e. £150 grossed up). The donor will himself claim the higher tax relief of £30, thus reducing the cost to him to £120. If the donor also pays investment income surcharge the figures are even more startling. This concession, as has been stated above, is subject to a £3,000 annual tax relief for each individual.

Deeds of covenant may be made 'gross' rather than net. In this case the donor names the gross amount which the PCC will receive, including the tax reclaimed. If he makes a gross deed for £1 when tax is at 25 per cent, he gives the PCC 75p and the PCC gets the remaining 25p back from the Inland Revenue. If tax goes up to 50 per cent, he drops his contribution to the PCC to 50p and the PCC claims 50p from the State; thus for a gross deed, it is the donor's amount which fluctuates and the PCC's which remains constant. The difficulty with this deed is that the donor's contribution varies each time there is a change in tax rates, so it is not really suitable for weekly or monthly contributions.

A PCC which has not taken full advantage of deeds of covenant is losing a very great deal of potential income. If only 50 people in the parish covenanted £2 per week, with tax at 25p in the pound, the PCC could reclaim £1,733 in a full year.

Loan or deposited covenants

A loan covenant (sometimes also known as a deposited covenant) is an arrangement by which the covenantor pays over to the PCC a single lump sum equal to all the payments which will become due over the life of the covenant. A deposited amount of, say, £400 in one lump sum means that the donor should sign a deed of covenant for £100 per annum for four years, provided that payment is not made before the covenant is signed, and the PCC will reclaim tax on the annual amount after the dates on which the payments are due, at the appropriate basic rate during the four years of the covenant.

Loan or deposited covenants must be covered by a carefully worded letter (see Appendix 5 for a sample) stating the terms and the amounts of the repayments.

Payroll giving

Some employers are willing to operate a Payroll Giving Scheme for their employees. If this facility is available, employees authorize the employer to deduct specified gifts from their pay, and nominate the charities which they wish to receive their gifts; employers give their employees tax relief by deducting gifts from pay before calculating the PAYE tax due; the employers pay the gift to an agency, which acts as a clearing house and which distributes the gifts to individual charities.

Under the Finance Act 1990 the upper limit on gifts qualifying for tax relief under this scheme was increased to £600 per annum (£50 per month).

Charities Aid Foundation

There are many people who like to give to a number of charities or respond to many appeals, yet who do not wish to covenant to all of them individually, because that would involve them in a plethora of deeds of covenant, all for different amounts and all expiring on different dates. They may be considerably helped by the Charities Aid Foundation (see p. 119). CAF is a registered charity which exists to serve other charities. The donor enters into a deed of covenant with CAF for a stated amount, and pays this amount by banker's order (either annually, quarterly, or monthly, so long as each payment is for a minimum of £25). CAF then issue him with a book of 'charity credits' which he uses like cheques, paying them out as he wishes to the charities of his choice whenever he feels like it. CAF reclaims the tax which has been deducted (around £33 for every £100 covenanted) and adds that to the donor's account. There are three stipulations: he cannot be overdrawn, but can only sign credits up to the amount he has in his account with CAF; the credits cannot be made out to individuals but only to charities (PCCs are charities for this purpose even though they are not individually registered); the CAF makes a deduction (currently 3 per cent of the gross value, i.e. £4 per annum on £100 plus £33) to help finance its parent body, the National Council for Voluntary Organizations. The remaining £129 or so is available for him to distribute by charity credit or standing order, as and when he likes, to the individual charities of his choice without the need for separate covenants.

Administration of deeds of covenant

A parochial set of deeds of covenant can easily be administered by any competent person who is prepared to learn a few necessary details. It is important, however, that he should be efficient and accurate, and that the claims are submitted each year. Parishes are known where covenants have been signed, but the tax has never been reclaimed because the person responsible has fallen down on the job. If this is likely to be the case, or if the number of deeds is so large that it is not possible to find a person with time enough to do it all, it is worth paying a fee to have the covenants professionally administered. Several dioceses are now offering parishes a centrally administered scheme for doing all the paper work. They may make a small charge to cover their costs. All that the parish has to do is to receive certificates from time to time which have to be signed by donors (or their executors) and returned to the diocesan office. Some dioceses may do this work themselves, in which case they will administer deeds made out in favour of PCCs.

The rest of this section, however, assumes that a volunteer in the parish will do the necessary administration. We will call him the recorder.

The PCC needs formally to appoint him as the person authorized to make repayment claims on its behalf and it must register this fact in its minutes. The recorder then writes to the Inland Revenue Claims branch informing them that the PCC is receiving income under deeds of covenant and enclosing a certified copy of the minute of the PCC whereby he has been appointed recorder. He should, in the same letter, ask for the following forms and certificates:

R 68 (Inland Revenue Tax Claim).
A supply of forms R 185(AP) – certificates for signature by donors.
Forms R 248A (for more than 50 deeds) and R 248B (for a smaller number) plus R 248A (summary) will be required if the shortened procedure is to be adopted for the second and subsequent years, in the case of amounts of under £400.
A grossing table for the current rate of income tax.

The forms include instructions for their use, but the diocesan stewardship adviser will always be ready to give help in their interpretation if asked.

The recorder should keep a register in which all the details of the deeds are recorded. This can most conveniently be done in a multi-column cash book. A specimen sheet for such a register is set out in Appendix 4 (see pp. 104–6 below).

This book will provide, at a glance, all the information about current deeds and payments.

Each claim should normally be made for an income tax year (6 April to 5 April), and involves the donor (or his executor) signing a certificate R 185(AP) for each of his current deeds of covenant. This covers the payments which have become due under the deed in question during the tax year and which have been received by the PCC. If payment is made by weekly, quarterly, or monthly instalments, the first and last claims may, in some cases, not relate to a full year but only to the period from the first payment to 5 April, or from 6 April to the final payment. The certificates should be signed in good time for the claim to be sent off immediately after 5 April. If there are many covenants, or if the amounts involved are large, more than one claim can be made each year.

The R 185(AP) certifies that the donor has paid the appropriate amount to the PCC during the tax year. If, however, the net annual amount is £400 or less, it is only necessary for the donor to sign the certificate for the first year of his covenant. If that is the case, the recorder must keep adequate records to prove that the appropriate amount has in fact been received. The books must be available for examination by the Inland Revenue if they ask for them. Before the shortened procedure is adopted, the Inland Revenue Claims Branch must be informed that the PCC wishes to adopt it. Note that when a form R 185(AP) is signed, the accuracy of the information thereon is the responsibility of the covenantor who signs it. If there is no R 185(AP), it is the recorder's responsibility to see that the claim is accurate.

If the full amount covenanted has not been received in any one year, the claim should be only for that proportion which has actually been received by the PCC, not the full amount of the covenant. If a compensating overpayment is made in a subsequent year, it is not possible to claim for any amount over and above the covenanted sum.

Each year, the recorder should send to the Inland Revenue Claims Branch the following:

R 68;
R 185(AP) – one signed by each covenantor or, if no R 185(AP) is needed, R 248A or B;
the original deeds of covenant – for the first claim only on each deed;
a copy of the parochial accounts for the last complete financial year.

When the recorder receives repayment from the Inland Revenue the amounts in respect of each deed and the date will be entered in his register. This will enable any new recorder to take over the books with the minimum of difficulty.

Set out in detail like this, it may sound complicated and time-consuming. In fact it is not. Most of the work falls to be done at the end of the tax year and, for most parishes, a few hours' work each year is all it needs. The rewards to the parish can be substantial, and when the cheque arrives from the Inland Revenue the recorder will feel a great glow of satisfaction at having done so much for the parish finances with so little expenditure of time and trouble.

Gift Aid (single gifts by individuals)

This is an entirely new method of giving introduced in the 1990 budget. It enables a donor (as from 1 October 1990) to give *as a single gift* £600 or more (maximum limit £5m) in any tax year. The PCC can then reclaim tax in one lump sum at the basic rate (currently 25 per cent), so increasing the value of the gift.

So a £600 single payment enables the PCC to reclaim £200 – total benefit to PCC is £800; or a £1,200 gift will enable the PCC to reclaim tax of £400. If the donor is a higher-rate taxpayer, he or she will get higher-rate relief – thus, on a donation of £600 the cost to the donor will be only £480. The donor gets £120 higher-rate relief.

This relief will apply to outright gifts of money and not gifts in kind. The appropriate amount of the tax must have been paid by the donor to the Inland Revenue. Gifts which have already qualified for income tax relief, such as covenant payments or donations under the payroll giving scheme, will not qualify for the new relief, nor will bequests made by the donor on his or her death.

No legally binding document has to be signed prior to the making of the gift. The donor is only asked to sign a form R 190 (SD) to the effect that the gift is being made, and the PCC will complete form R 68 (Gift Aid Insert) in order to reclaim the tax. The forms are available from the Inland Revenue Claims Branch (see p. 119). R 190 (SD) is the only form permitted – photocopies will not be accepted.

The advantages of this method of giving are that the donor makes a single payment of £600 or more (either once only or from time to time) and as it does not involve a four-year promise, the PCC receives the full benefit almost immediately. This will be of advantage to PCCs trying to raise large sums of money in a short time for, say, expensive restoration work, new church building schemes etc.

7

Parochial Accounts and Budgets

In the earlier chapters of this book we have explained some of the peculiarities of parish accounts. Now it is time to put all these details together into the overall picture of how the parish treasurer operates.

When a new treasurer takes over, there will be many practical details he will want to know. If he can work for a while in collaboration with the former treasurer, much of this will be passed on at the appropriate time; but some of the information only crops up once a year, so ideally the new treasurer should work 'in tandem' with his predecessor for a whole financial year so that he can see what happens at various stages. This is sometimes quite impossible. Treasurers may leave the district at short notice. Sometimes they can fall ill and be unable to share the work with a successor or to explain it to him. Sometimes (alas) they may die in office. In emergencies (as has been stated above – p. 2) a churchwarden may need to take over unexpectedly.

For all these reasons, it is most helpful if the treasurer keeps the books up to date at all times. A 'treasurer's notebook' is also invaluable. This (which can most conveniently be loose-leaf) contains general information and also a check-list diary month by month of matters which need attention at particular times of the year. The use of a book such as this will greatly simplify the task of handing over and taking over the treasurership, as well as being a useful *aide-mémoire* to the person who has compiled it. The general pages would contain such information as:

name and address of bank;
bank's code number;
full title(s) and code number(s) of parochial account(s);
details and whereabouts of stock certificates, loan documents, etc.;

names and addresses of persons authorized to sign cheques on behalf of PCC or subsidiary accounts;

how many signatures are needed on cheques;
   (a) below £...,
   (b) above £...;

name and address of auditor;

name and address of covenant recorder;

name and address of stewardship recorder (if different from the above);

names and addresses (and telephone numbers) of diocesan officials whom it has been found useful to consult;

names and addresses of charities customarily supported by the PCC;

copies (with dates) of any relevant PCC minutes authorizing opening of bank accounts or treasurer's procedures, etc.;

the whereabouts of the safe custody receipt for any silver, deeds, stock certificates, etc. deposited at the bank (together with the name and address of the bank concerned);

details (with amounts and due dates) of banker's orders (credits and debits).

In addition there will usefully be a page of information which needs to be checked through every month. Each parish will need a different one, but the following is a sample of what monthly pages might contain:

working expenses
   – incumbent,
   – assistant staff;
caretaker's pay;
organist's pay;
tax due to Collector of Taxes;
instalment of diocesan quota/share;
instalment of contribution to diocesan stipends fund;
other monthly banker's orders.

It is useful to have banker's orders listed here so that the treasurer can see from this list and his paying-in book and cheque stubs what his current balance is – standing order payments are easy to overlook and can lead to overdrawing or unnecessary bank charges.

Then there will be a series of pages, one for each calendar month throughout the year, on which some of the above information could be repeated. Again, each parish's details will be different, but these are the kinds of things that might feature in such a list:

January
Close accounts for year ending 31 December.
Take all necessary documentation to auditor.

Ascertain date of annual parochial church meeting.
Make diary notes of dates when:
    (a) copy of parish accounts to be posted on church door(s),
    (b) signed copy of approved accounts to be posted up.
Prepare budget (if not done in October or November)

February
Present audited accounts to PCC at this month's meeting.
Interest due from CBF Deposit Fund.
Electricity bill due.
Banker's order £... to diocese for quarter's Parish Share.

March
Gas bill due.
Prepare copies of annual accounts for annual parochial church meeting.
Put copy of accounts on church door(s) at least seven days before APCM.

April
After APCM, put signed copy of agreed accounts on church door(s).
Prepare income tax certificates R 185(AP) for deeds of covenant for signature by donors, then (when they are signed) send off tax repayment claim to Inland Revenue Claims Branch (or remind recorder to do so).
Prepare and send off any necessary tax repayment claim for tax deducted at source on dividends, local authority mortgages, tax deducted by solicitors on any legacy or part of residuary estate, etc. (or remind recorder).
Telephone bill due.

May
Dividend on stock due from Bank of England (gross £..., net amount credited to bank direct. Interest to be used for maintenance of church and churchyard according to terms of Pennyfeather bequest).
Banker's order £... to diocese.
Electricity bill due.

June
Gas bill due.
Insurance premium due.
Repayment of loan of £... to ... for church restoration (annually for 15 years from 1988; originally £3,000 at 8 per cent).

July etc. etc.

An additional benefit of this kind of monthly check-list is to help cash flow by noting the months in which heavy bills come due for payment, so that money can be withdrawn in time (e.g. for the gas bill if the church is on gas-fired central heating), or put on deposit if it is not going to be needed immediately.

General and methods

The person who takes on the administration of PCC accounts, takes on a deal of responsibility. So does anyone who takes over the accounts of any organization, be it tennis club or amateur operatic society; but there are additional constraints in the case of the parish treasurer. A tennis club probably exists only for the sake of its own members, and involves no linked clubs or organizations within which it has legally-binding links as well as family loyalties. The PCC is different. The treasurer does not have a free hand in what he does. He is the servant of the PCC (even though, as we have seen on p. 2 above, his appointment must be an honorary one) and the PCC is subject to specific statutes and measures as well as to the ordinary law of the land. All money passing through the PCC's care, and all money put on to the collection plate in church, becomes trust money, to be used for religious and charitable purposes in accordance with the laws relating to trust funds. The treasurer is responsible to the trust for keeping its cash books and other documents accurately and in seemly order.

Of the papers handed over by the old treasurer, or generated by the new one in due course, all cash books should be kept permanently. The current one and the immediate past one will be needed for use and reference; the older ones should be kept in the church safe or other place of custody. Vouchers should be retained for a period of six years, after which it is safe to destroy them. (This refers to paying-in slips, bank statements, cheque stubs and the like, and receipted bills.)

For everyone's protection, all transactions should be made (so far as possible) by cheque or bank transfer. This means that all movements of money are recorded and anyone who has a right to do so can see from the books exactly what is happening. This is desirable, not because there is much suspicion of dishonesty (that, fortunately, is extremely rare), but so that everything may be open and above board and that anyone who wishes to make enquiries can be assured that no money is being misappropriated. It protects voluntary helpers, and guards against that kind of well-meaning sloppiness by which so many small voluntary accounts get into a hopeless muddle.

There will, of course, need to be a petty cash float, and the incumbent or church official should have authority to buy small items and be reimbursed in cash or by cheque. But all such transactions should be recorded and based upon written petty cash vouchers (pads of which are available from most stationers), accompanied by receipts where possible. The vouchers will be kept to be examined by the auditor at the year's end. Again, if an official is allowed a cash float he should keep an account of amounts received and expended, and should submit statements from time to time to the treasurer with vouchers attached, so that the treasurer has the information for audit purposes.

Many regular payments may be made by standing order, credit transfer, or direct debit. These need no cheque, letter, envelope, or stamp, and save a great deal of time and expense. The treasurer, however, needs to keep an eye on them if he wants to maintain a proper cash flow – it is easy to forget about them and run up an expensive overdraft unnecessarily.

When a new treasurer is appointed (or a new bank account opened) the bank will ask for a mandate from the PCC, signed by two or three members, certifying the relevant PCC minute. (Forms for this are available from most branches of all banks.) This will state who may sign cheques. The treasurer will hold the cheque book, so he is an obvious signatory; but in case he is ill or away there ought to be alternative names – the incumbent, churchwardens or PCC secretary. Many PCCs make the stipulation that cheques should bear two signatures. A useful variation is to allow cheques under a certain amount (£100?) to be signed by the treasurer alone, but for larger sums to need two signatories (blank cheques should not be signed in advance). All this is at the discretion of the PCC and should be decided and minuted before the mandate is sent to the bank.

Church collections should be counted as soon after the service as possible, and recorded in the service register immediately (the register should be kept in the vestry, not in the parsonage). It is usual for collections to be divided into 'loose cash' and 'envelope offerings'. These latter need to be opened and recorded separately (see under Stewardship, p. 66). Procedures vary from parish to parish but the incumbent, treasurer, and PCC should satisfy themselves that the methods adopted are as efficient as possible.

As soon as the collections and contents of stewardship envelopes have been counted and recorded and their accuracy verified, they should be bagged ready for the bank and put into the church safe overnight. In many areas, particularly in towns, it is possible to put money into the night safe at the bank if arrangements have been made in advance. Every effort should be made to avoid having parish money overnight (or even during the day) in a private house.

It is an added risk, and may not be covered by the insurance policy (see p. 52 above).

All money should be banked as soon as possible – preferably on Monday morning. This does not need to be the treasurer's chore. He may need to delegate it, particularly if his work does not permit him to make a weekday journey to the bank.

When PCC money is banked, the person doing so should make sure that the counterfoil of the paying-in slip, or the paying-in book, states the source of the money paid in – for example 'Cash and envelope collections 21 June 1991', or 'magazine sales January 1991' or 'proceeds of coffee morning at 24 High Street', etc. This is a useful cross check, and – more importantly – if money is paid in by persons other than the treasurer, the counterfoil allows him immediately to know to which part of the accounts to enter the credit. Without the counterfoil, he may simply get (some time later) a bank statement with an amount marked 'sundries', and might waste a great deal of time on detective work before he finds out who paid it in and for what purpose.

After money has been paid in, the paying-in slip or book (with the bank's stamp on it) should be returned to the treasurer so that he can enter the amounts in his books. Alternatively, it may be put back into the church safe to be collected by the treasurer when he wants it for making up the books.

Large sums of money should never be left in a current account where they will earn no interest – though the balance kept in the account should always be large enough to ensure that anticipated withdrawals do not cause an overdraft and attract interest charges. Most banks waive charges for transactions if a minimum balance is maintained in the account. It is important to find out from the bank what their arrangements are in respect of charges, and to work the account in such a way as to minimize charges and maximize earnings. Any amount over and above immediate needs should be transferred to a deposit account. If the sum is not needed for some months, better interest rates can be obtained from the Central Board of Finance Deposit Fund (see p. 27, above). This is certainly the best procedure if money is being received in advance for an anticipated capital expenditure (for a new building or a restoration scheme, for example) or if a legacy has been received and it is likely to be some time before the PCC has decided how to spend it.

Overdrafts on PCC accounts are not illegal, but they are expensive and not to be encouraged. It is unwise to allow an overdraft to run for more than a month without informing the PCC. If capital work is being done and bills need to be paid before grants are paid from outside sources, arrangements should be made with the bank for an overdraft to cover this contingency. Evidence that the grants are promised and certain will usually need to be given before over-draft facilities are authorized. Overdrafts should not be allowed to grow, nor to drag on longer than absolutely necessary.

How many bank accounts?

Some PCCs like to have a multiplicity of separate bank accounts, each dealing with one section of parish business – a general account for the PCC, separate accounts for daughter churches, a magazine account, a fabric fund, different accounts for the parish hall lettings, and Sunday school. In this case, each account will have its own cheque book and bank statements; some accounts could have different signatories from others; some accounts can be fed from others by regular credits and thereafter preserve their autonomy within the budget allocated. All the separate accounts will be subject to annual audit, and their transactions summarized in the annual accounts of the PCC.

There may be occasions on which this may be desirable or necessary – it may give freedom of decision to a district church council looking after a daughter church where the annual parochial church meeting has decided to delegate day-to-day management functions. But before too easily acquiescing in the request to multiply separate bank accounts, consider the snags. It can create difficulties and misunderstandings as to who is actually responsible for which accounts, and who is authorized by whom to initiate expenditure. It can complicate the work of the treasurer if he has many sub-accounts to administer and sub-treasurers responsible to him. If money is raised for some parochial purpose it is generally more satisfactory to have it handed over to the parish treasurer so that members of the PCC are fully aware of all items of income and expenditure appertaining to the church. This is particularly true if the sum is earmarked for some particular purpose. Little sub-accounts salted away by particular groups can cause troubles, especially if the PCC thereby gets the impression that there is parish money over which it has no adequate control.

If a member of the congregation has a bring and buy sale, a coffee morning or some other function to raise money for, say, church kneelers, new hymn books, church repairs or missionary work, the proceeds should be given to the treasurer or paid into the PCC account, so that the council is aware of all that is being done in the name of the Church by members of the congregation. If the money has been raised for a specific purpose, then the PCC will have to ensure that it is used for that purpose. This procedure enables a PCC to be in effective control, and not – for instance – to find someone producing new hymn books, the use of which has not been approved. It also helps to avoid difficulties and misunderstandings which might, on occasions, arise.

To have a single composite PCC account under the control of one treasurer may also, on occasions, avoid bank charges or an overdraft. One section may well be in temporary deficit, but generally other sections will be in credit so that, overall, no financial penalty is incurred. It is easy (see below) for the treasurer to use an account book with a multi-column analysis lay-out so that all the PCC's financial affairs are contained within the one bank account.

A limited number of exceptions to this general rule may be in order. For example, the Mothers' Union or uniformed organizations may be required to submit their accounts to national headquarters. These are frequently separately administered by a member of the group or organization concerned. If at any time financial help is requested from the PCC it may ask to see a copy of the latest annual account of the group. However, if such a group raises money specifically for a parochial purpose, it should pass from the group's account to the PCC treasurer and be recorded in the PCC accounts.

There is, however, one statutory exception. If there is a vacancy in the benefice and when there is a sequestration account, this account must be kept separate. It is a benefice account, not a PCC account, and it is administered by those authorized in the Writ of Sequestration to see to benefice finances during the vacancy. The sequestrators will normally include the two churchwardens – not, generally, the PCC treasurer as such. Since the coming into operation of the Endowments and Glebe Measure 1976, the financial work of sequestrators has considerably reduced. In many cases the only moneys they receive on behalf of the benefice are the fees payable to the incumbent for occasional offices (e.g. weddings and funerals). Each diocese will issue its own instructions to the sequestrators, and no money ought to be paid out, nor should the account be closed at the end of the vacancy, without studying and understanding these instructions, or without enquiring of the diocesan office.

Account book

There is no statutory provision governing the type of account book which should be kept. Some treasurers prefer to keep their accounts on scraps of paper (even on the backs of envelopes), but such treasurers should be quietly replaced as soon as possible.

A very small parish with the minimum of transactions might be able to get by with a cash book showing income on one side and expenditure on the other, and no more than a single column of figures on either side of the book; but the most satisfactory way is to have a multi-column cash book with headings approximating to the main budget headings. In this way it is much more easy to extract figures at the end of the year for the annual accounts, but it is also very useful for keeping a watch on the figures during the year, so that if income or expenditure is very different from the expectations as forecast in the budget, a PCC can be alerted to the fact.

For years, the Central Board of Finance has produced a book giving a standard form of parochial accounts, which has been adopted by many parish treasurers. The use of this book is strongly recommended. Its current form is as the *Parochial Church Accounts Book* (1987 edition), loose-leaf, and in a ring binder, available from Church House Bookshop, 31 Great Smith Street, London SW1P 3BN. Prices (1991) are £20.85 for the book and £14.75 per pack of 100 refill sheets – both prices including VAT and postage. The headings are printed (thus avoiding constant rewriting). When treasurers are asked by the CBF to complete their statistical return, their task will be that much more simple since the figures asked for in the return refer to the columns of the Account Book. The book contains a model budget, a sample income and expenditure account, and a sample balance sheet of funds and property held (reproduced in Appendix 6, on pp. 108–12 below). Its contents are:

notes on parochial church accounts;
notes on statutory provisions affecting parochial church accounts;
cash and analysis sections, with examples showing how they should
  be kept;
record sections:
  current investments,
  permanent investments and property,
  insurance;
specimens and blank pages:
  income and expenditure accounts,
  permanent investments and property,
  budget.

The treasurer should make up his accounts regularly (at least monthly). The bank could be asked to send a statement automatically made up to the last day of each month. The treasurer should reconcile his accounts with the statement each time it arrives (see Appendix 8). If any cheques are still outstanding after (say) three months, a letter should be sent to the payee, since cheques cannot be presented later than six months from their original dating.

Income

At its most simple, parochial income could consist of two main items – collections and fees. Under 'collections' are included cash, envelopes, tax recovered, donations, etc., and 'fees' will be dealt with in a later paragraph.

Most parishes, however, will have additional sources of income. Many will have a parish hall which is let at a charge; most have a parish magazine which provides a certain amount of income from sales and advertising revenue; some are fortunate enough to have legacies; in some there are trust funds under the control of the PCC for specific purposes; occasionally there are investments made from past savings or endowments; and there can be few parishes which do not have coffee mornings, summer fetes, autumn bazaars, jumble sales or other 'fund-raising' functions. The parochial accounts can reveal a great deal about the parish. Are the 'special events' the financial lifeline of the parish? Is the regular giving of the committed congregation sufficient to keep the wheels turning? Or does the church have to rely on the impulse buying of the less-committed well-wishers who are persuaded along to a fund-raising event? What is the relationship of special efforts to missionary giving? Some parishes insist that any special efforts should help cement the social and fellowship aspects of the life of the congregation (and this should never be despised – fetes can be great fun), but that any proceeds accruing from them should go outside the parish to some missionary or charitable cause. That is splendid, so long as an adequate amount *does* thereby go out of the parish – and we shall have more to say about that under the 'expenditure' section later in this chapter. What the parish must *not* do is regard the parish share or parish quota to the diocese as 'charitable giving' in this sense. It is not; it is part of the inescapable commitment of being part of a larger family.

If the parish has income from specific trusts, care should be taken to ascertain the terms of these trusts, and to comply with them. If there is doubt as to whether certain payments fall within the orbit of a particular trust, the diocesan solicitors are usually willing and able to give advice.

No further explanation is required about most of the items marked 'income' in parish accounts, except for three matters – legacies, fees, and alms and collections. We deal with them in reverse order.

Alms and collections

The rubric within the Communion Service of the Book of Common Prayer, which provides that 'the money given at the Offertory shall be disposed of to such pious and charitable uses, as the Minister and Churchwardens shall think fit', has been modified by the Church of England (Legal Aid and Miscellaneous Provisions) Measure 1988.

It is now the joint responsibility of minister and PCC to determine the objects for which all moneys collected in church are to be given, as stated in Section 7(iv) of the Parochial Church Councils (Powers) Measure 1956, as amended by the 1988 Measure. In cases where minister and PCC cannot agree, Section 9(3) of the 1956 Measure provides that the bishop shall direct the way in which the matter shall be dealt with.

There is nothing to prevent the PCC agreeing with the incumbent to put all or part of the moneys collected at any service into a separate 'Incumbent's Discretionary Fund' which he may use for charitable giving at his discretion. The diocesan authorities should be consulted about the relation of this to assessments for diocesan share or quota – missionary and charitable donations are sometimes exempted from such calculations by those dioceses which base quota assessments on parish income.

If there is a collection at any service, and it is announced beforehand that it is to be for a specific charitable purpose, then it becomes trust money which must be applied for that purpose and no other.

In some parishes, the custom of allocating the collections on Easter Day to the incumbent is still in force. In nearly every case, there is now no purpose served by doing so. The incumbent has to declare the amount received to the diocese. Unless his benefice income is so large that he receives no augmentation grant from the diocese (and this is the case in very few parishes) the diocese will then adjust his augmentation by an amount equivalent to that received from the Easter Offering, so that at the end of the day he is no better off. All that will have happened is that the diocesan stipends fund benefits by the amount given to the incumbent. It is far better, therefore, for the collection to be honestly and openly designated as 'For the Diocesan Stipends Fund'; the givers are not then under the misapprehension that their generosity is having any direct effect on the stipend of the incumbent.

Where Easter Offerings are made to the incumbent (or Whitsun offerings to assistant staff), the sum given must be declared to the Diocesan Office and the Inspector of Taxes. It will not be regarded as a tax-free gift, but as part of the emoluments received by reason of the office held by the minister in question, and therefore taxable.

Fees

The Ecclesiastical Fees Measure 1986 lays down that fees are payable to incumbents and to PCCs in connection with the performance of certain duties. Their amounts are fixed from time to time by Fees Orders, which are drawn up by the Church Commissioners, debated and passed by the General Synod, and laid before Parliament for ratification. Copies of Fees Orders are sent to incumbents when they are first published, and duplicate copies may be obtained on request from the Church Commissioners.

Fees income – obviously – varies enormously from parish to parish. When it is small, the PCC may well be content to allow it to form part of its normal income and not be specially earmarked. When it is considerable there is much to be said for setting at least part of it aside towards (for instance) a Church Fabric Fund or other special purpose.

There are many fees which are commonly charged which are not laid down in the table of fees in the Fees Order. They are a matter for negotiation between the incumbent and the parties concerned. It is better if the amounts are laid down from time to time by the PCC, or even agreed on a deanery or diocesan basis, and then the incumbent cannot be accused of acting arbitrarily. The PCC would also agree under what circumstances to give the incumbent the right to waive a fee. Fees not covered by any statutory or local authority order include payments for music (organist, choristers, and bell-ringers); payments for furnishings and flowers; charges for specially heating the church (over and above what would be normally done at that particular hour) for a wedding or special service; payments made in connection with TV or radio recordings; fees charged for allowing photographs or video recordings to be taken in church; postal searches or other searches undertaken on behalf of an enquirer not specifically covered in the Fees Order; special services (e.g. memorial services) and the like.

Legacies

The Church has reason to be grateful to those who in the past have left money to it. Without the permanent results of such giving, we would be hard put to it to maintain the ministry and services we now do. Such cushioning is – of course – a mixed blessing in that it may leave the living church complacent about its financial responsibilities for the furtherance of the Gospel. In recent years, members of the Church of England have had to wake up to the fact that inherited wealth can no longer support the Church, and that an increasing proportion of its expenditure has to come from its living and worshipping congregations. This is all to the good, but we should never despise legacies, and from time to time members of the Church should be reminded that they ought to remember the Church in their own will. Too many Christians refuse to face the fact that death is an inevitability which needs to be prepared for in a Christian way. There is an embarrassed conspiracy of silence about it, and even preachers who dare to make death the subject of their discourse are often criticized for being 'morbid'. They are not – they are being realistic, and reminding their congregation that, since Christ has drawn the sting of death, they can look the facts of death in the face without fear. Many people (even, it must be said to their shame, many ministers) do not make a will at all, and for this there is no excuse. Christians do not have to be particularly wealthy to be able to leave some of their possessions to the Church in their will.

When doing so, it is advisable to discuss the matter with one's solicitor. Legacies which are hedged in with too many conditions can be a burden rather than a help to a parish church. A badly-worded legacy can cost the parish a great deal in lawyers' fees (even on occasion necessitating Counsel's Opinion) to determine what the testator really meant and whether a certain proposed allocation of the legacy is within the terms laid down. Nevertheless, if conditions are laid down they must be strictly adhered to, because a legacy is a trust. Legacies left 'For the furtherance of the religious and charitable work of the Parish of X in such ways as the Incumbent and PCC see fit' can be of tremendous value in enabling the Church to embark on some pioneer work which might otherwise be impossible; but the testator must be able to trust the incumbent and PCC enough to lay down so wide a definition of the purposes. It is possible to include some such wording as 'for the evangelistic work of the parish' or 'for educational purposes within the parish' or 'for purposes connected with the maintenance or extension of the fabric of the parish church building', but all these phrases are of doubtful interpretation, and should be resisted if possible. If one's own solicitor is not an expert in ecclesiastical law (and few are) it may be wise to ask the diocesan solicitor or the diocesan registrar for advice.

Missionary and charitable giving

Many items of expenditure on a parish budget are self-explanatory. Others have been dealt with in detail in the earlier chapters of this Handbook. But so far nothing has been said about the item usually headed 'Missionary and Charitable Giving'. Often we are well enough aware of the need to ask individuals to give to the Church through the PCC, yet tragically blind to the need for the PCC itself to look beyond its own immediate needs and its own boundaries to the needs of the wider Church and to all humanity. Too many parish budgets are quite sinfully inward-looking, and the PCC which can easily be persuaded that gas and electricity bills must be paid and the church building kept clean and tidy and properly equipped (even that the insurances must be paid and the ministers' expenses need to be provided) shuts its eyes when the wider Church is mentioned. Well-worn slogans like 'charity begins at home' are trotted out, or the PCC is told that 'we would like to give to missions, but if we did we could not keep our own plant going', or 'it is for individual church members to give to the charities of their choice, not for the PCC to do their charitable giving for them'. None of these excuses will wash. Just as an individual's Christian credibility rests upon whether he is prepared to back his profession of faith by his acts – and by the disposition of his possessions – so the credibility of the PCC as a Christian body rests upon whether it spends all its money on self or whether its eyes are open to the needs of humanity.

Many parishes teach that their congregation should tithe (either literally by giving a tenth of their income away, or metaphorically by setting aside some lesser percentage of their disposable wealth). On this principle, a PCC should aim to give away no less a percentage of the parish budget. Some do this by ensuring that there are sales of work or gift days specially devoted to missionary giving. Others ensure that the tithe is met first and sales of work are additional offerings. Some parishes are known to give away half their income (and that does not include the diocesan share or quota, which must not be counted as 'missionary giving' but as bearing the parish's due share of necessary centralized expenditure). If a parish is asking members of the congregation to be good stewards of their money, the PCC in its turn must likewise not spend all its income on its own internal needs. These principles must be borne in mind when the budget is being drawn up.

The means of distribution of the PCC tithe needs to be carefully thought out. It is all too easy to have a list of charities customarily supported, and to divide the amount available in the same proportions year by year as an agenda item taking up less than five minutes of the PCC's time each year. In that way, the charities may be materially supported, but the understanding of the congregation and its commitment to the work it thereby supports is minimal. There must be information and education, so that the congregation knows something of the work of the missions and charities supported. Some missionary societies provide 'link persons' who correspond with supporting parishes and send personal news and pictures, even tape-recorded messages. The PCC needs to discuss means by which the congregation may become aware of the realities behind PCC donations, and means by which the congregational awareness may be fed back to the PCC in order to affect the pattern of PCC giving. That may take more time than passing last year's list 'on the nod' at budget time, but it is time worth giving.

Audit

The Church Representation Rules state in Rule 5 that 'the annual meeting [i.e. the annual parochial church meeting which has to be held in every parish not later than 30 April each year] shall appoint the auditors to the council'. Appendix 2 to Rule 13 states that 'if auditors to the council are not appointed by the annual meeting, or if auditors appointed by the annual meeting are unable or unwilling to act, auditors (who shall not be members of the council) shall be appointed by the council. The remuneration (if any) of the auditors shall be paid by the council'.

The Rules make no reference as to whether the auditor should be professionally qualified. It is for the parish to determine whether to appoint a professional auditor or firm of accountants, who will charge their fee, or whether to rely on a friendly volunteer with sufficient financial expertise to carry it out as a labour of love. Much depends upon the size and complexity of the accounts and whether or not a suitable volunteer can be found. If a professional fee is likely to be incurred, the auditors should be asked in advance for an estimated figure. The annual meeting and/or the PCC should be asked to bear this in mind when making the appointment, though if it has been previous practice to employ a paid auditor, his last year's fee may be shown in the annual accounts and the treasurer will already have inserted a figure in the proposed budget for the year.

As soon as the books for the year have been closed, the treasurer will need to send or take to the auditor all the papers he will need in order to carry out his audit. This will include the cash book(s), receipted bills, paying-in slips or book, bank statements, cheque stubs or returned cheques, deposit account statement, dividend statements, interest statements etc. It is not for the auditor to prepare an income and expenditure account or statement of funds and property held. That is the treasurer's job. The auditor's function is to check those statements, to see that all items purporting to have been paid have in fact been paid, that all items purporting to have been received have indeed been received, and that payments which have been made have been properly authorized.

When the auditor is satisfied that the accounts are correct and complete, and in accordance with the vouchers and receipts he has examined, he will sign some such statement at the foot of the accounts as 'We have examined the foregoing receipts and payments accounts for the year ending 31 December 19.. (and the statement of funds and property held as at that date) with the books and vouchers and certify the same to be correct and in accordance therewith'.

The audited accounts are then posted on or near the church door, and presented to the annual parochial church meeting (see below). The PCC will have seen copies of these accounts and should have discussed them and their implications with the treasurer at a meeting between the end of the financial year and the public presentation of the accounts.

The Annual Parochial Church Meeting

The presentation of the accounts at the annual parochial church meeting is governed by the Parochial Church Councils (Powers) Measure 1956 and the Church Representation Rules. The APCM must be held not later than 30 April. Section 8 of the PCC (Powers) Measure contains the provisions that:

(1) Every council shall furnish to the annual church meeting the audited accounts of the council for the year ending on the 31st December immediately preceding the meeting and an audited statement of the funds and property, if any, remaining in the hands of the council at that date ...

(4) The accounts of all trusts administered by the council shall be laid before the diocesan authority annually.

Within Rule 8 of the Church Representation Rules, the following provisions relate to the presentation of accounts at the APCM:

8 (1) The annual meeting shall receive from the parochial church council and shall be free to discuss: – ...

(c) an annual report on the financial affairs of the parish;

(d) the audited accounts of the parochial church council for the year ending on the 31st December immediately preceding the meeting;

(e) an audited statement of the funds and property, if any, remaining in the hands of the parochial church council at the said date; ...

(2) The council shall cause a copy of the said audited accounts and the said audited statement to be affixed on or near the principal door of every church in the parish and every building licensed for public worship in the parish at least seven days before the annual meeting.

(3) Such accounts and statement shall be submitted to the annual meeting for approval. If approved, they shall be signed by the chairman of the meeting, who shall then deliver them to the parochial church council for publication, and the parochial church council shall forthwith cause them to be published and affixed for a period of at least fourteen days on or near the principal door of every church in the parish and every building licensed for public worship in the parish and at such other conspicuous place or places in the parish as the parochial church council think

appropriate, and shall cause a copy to be sent to the secretary of the diocesan board of finance.

The law would be complied with if the treasurer held the only copy of the accounts (which he had placed on the church door for seven days previously) and simply read the figures from them to the annual meeting. The meeting would be asked 'Any questions?' and if there were none, 'Do you approve of the accounts?'; the chairman would sign them and the signed copy would go back on to the church door again for fourteen days. That, however, would be a travesty. Nobody at the annual meeting can take in the significance of a mass of figures as they are read out. At the very least, the treasurer should see that copies of the accounts as audited are duplicated and made available to the APCM to examine. He should take the meeting through the main headings and point out their significance. It is helpful (and almost universally done) to print for comparison the corresponding figures for the previous year in a column parallel to the last year's figures, so that any changes can be immediately obvious and questions asked and explanations given.

Even this is not really enough, because many of those present at the APCM will not be sufficiently familiar with figures and numbers to take in the significance of a column of them. The treasurer may want to include with the accounts a supplementary statement showing what percentage of income and expenditure is represented by each item. The meeting then knows, without having to calculate it, whether the PCC has given 1 per cent or 50 per cent of its income to missions and charities, or whether the heating of the church and premises accounts for 10 or 75 per cent of the total. The percentage increase in the totals between the last year and the previous one can usefully be given, and compared with the Retail Price Index as published by the government. In that way, the congregation can see whether its income and giving are keeping pace with inflation, or whether an apparent increase in giving represents a fall in real purchasing power. At times a comparative chart showing trends over a number of years may be useful, since particular years may not be typical. The visual chart – a circle divided into segments, or a £5 note cut up into pieces, or a row of 10p coins showing how much of each £1 received came from what source, and how much of each £1 spent went to each purpose – is even more revealing than a column of percentages. This kind of presentation helps many of the congregation who are better at visualizing than at abstract thinking. They can then see where the money comes from and where it goes. If the treasurer is not very good at this himself (or, particularly, if he is not himself helped by it, and thinks it ought to be beneath the dignity of the APCM) he ought to ask a friend who is good at visual aids to prepare some charts for him on the basis of the figures he can supply. He will probably be astonished at the way this contributes both to the ease with which, and to the depth at which, the APCM grasps the financial facts he wishes to get across to them.

Interpreting the figures

The income and expenditure account as presented to the APCM is a revealing document, and anyone who has had to examine a large number of them from many different parishes will soon find that he develops a 'nose' for them. They will tell him a great deal about what kind of parish it is, what kind of teaching has got home to the congregation, what kind of priorities the PCC adopts, and much else. On pp. 93–4 below are given four sets of figures from four different kinds of parish. Look at them and see what they tell you about the parishes concerned. They may not be typical – but they have lessons for all of us. They were compiled in 1980, so inflation has made the figures out of date; but the points we make still stand.

Parish A

This might be a village parish of population around 3,000, and a small congregation. There appears to be no planned giving scheme. There is not one deed of covenant, so there is no income from reclaimed tax. The income from sales of work, etc., is almost as great as that from church collections. Regular giving is low – £16 a week on average (how many families does this represent, we wonder? What is the average amount which each supporting family put on the plate each week? How much is this as a percentage of their disposable income?). The amount paid to the incumbent towards the working expenses of the church is low. £3 a week does not go far towards postages and telephone bills, let alone motoring – car licence and insurance will eat that up before the vicar has spent a penny on petrol. Nothing is given to overseas missions and there is no provision for the work of the Sunday school, lay training, or development. There were a few minor repairs to the buildings but no reserve built up to pay for quinquennial inspections and the work which such an inspection might reveal to be necessary. One has the impression that this parish lives from hand to mouth and meets crises when they occur (always hoping they won't).

Parish B

A town church serving a population of 11,000. There is a planned giving scheme, but no figure under 'tax recovered', so clearly there are no deeds of covenant or else no tax is being reclaimed from them.

Income

	Parish A	Parish B	Parish C	Parish D
Collections – cash	855	740	4,170	22,700
Planned giving incl. covenants		1,100	7,570	10,900
Tax recovered		400	1,900	5,200
Weddings & funerals				
Donations	23	20		9,100
Gift day		140		
Sales of work, bazaars, jumble sales etc.	830	1,109		
Missionary gift day			1,470	
Donations etc. earmarked for missions etc.			1,830	1,300
Fees	140	180	130	20
Magazine	40		200	120
Bookstall – tapes etc.			10	360
Investment income		260	40	300
Gifts earmarked for parish projects			770	
Rent of hall, land etc.		500	300	
Legacy			190	
From reserves for specific projects			1,300	
	£1,888	£4,449	£19,880	£50,000

Expenditure

	Parish A	Parish B	Parish C	Parish D
Incumbent – house	70	40	140	
Working expenses	150	650	1,940	2,100
Assistant minister honorarium		100	600	
Heating, lighting & cleaning	350	460	1,600	1,600
Insurance	180	120	530	370
Minor repairs	130	50	20	280
Property – rates & repairs			70	
Upkeep of services	40	120	730	
Organist	15	125	400	600
Lay training			30	
Sunday school			90	460
Church school		250		
Magazine	53	40	210	170
Administration/Secretarial help	74	190	590	2,600
Capital work			620	2,000
Payments out of parish:				
Diocese (quota, stipends, parsonage)	602	1,650	5,640	3,600
Missions		100	4,070	25,200
Home missions, societies etc.	55	90	660	7,200
Fellowship help				1,400
Loan interest repayment		300		
Fabric reserve account			2,000	
Development & outreach				2,500
	£1,719	£4,285	£19,940	£50,080

The planned giving does not produce a very significant proportion of parish income – cash collections and retiring collections at weddings and funerals together exceed the income from planned giving, and so does the income from sales of work and the like. On the expenditure side, we see that the amount paid towards working expenses is better than in Parish A, but it may be doubted whether it covers all that the incumbent has to spend on the work of the parish. The insurance premium looks low. Unless the church is unusually small for a town parish of that size, it is probably seriously under-insured. A look at past years' accounts will indicate whether the amount has been revised recently. We suspect it will prove to have been allowed to remain static rather a long time. The parish contributes towards an Aided school recently replaced by a new one. Expressed as a percentage of total income (4.4 per cent) the amount contributed to missions and charities is low. There is nothing for lay training or Sunday school work, development and outreach, nor any reserve fund. It is a parish which just about keeps ticking over; not a set of accounts to be proud of.

Parish C

A town centre church with a resident population of around 3,000 but attracting some eclectic congregation from outside the boundaries. Its deeds of covenant show how the church can benefit from re-claimed tax. There are no sales of work needed to balance the budget (expenditure is slightly above income, but by so small an amount that it will be put right next year). Gifts are earmarked for overseas work and there was a gift day for the same purpose. Together these raised £3,300, so a further £1,430 from parish funds was put into missions and charities. Parish income apart from the earmarked money and gift day proceeds was £16,580, so this parish gave 8.6 per cent of its income to missions and charities over and above earmarked donations and special efforts. Reimbursement of the incumbent's working expenses (including car running and depreciation costs) is more realistic. There is income from invest-ments and property, etc. There is a small amount for lay training and the Sunday school, but nothing for the church school (as it is a controlled one, this is not surprising) and nothing for development and outreach within the parish. It does, however, set aside money each year into a fabric fund, and there are reserves which can be called upon to meet emergency items.

Parish D

A town church whose population is only 2,500 but which draws a wide eclectic congregation from the rest of the town and from villages around. At one time it was threatened with closure, but a newly-appointed incumbent set to work to renew its ministry to congregation and parish. Commitment to mission and service was mirrored in financial commitment, and the result was obvious. It goes far beyond what we have been saying and recommending here. As a result of its secure financial situation, over half the parish income can be given to missions and charities. The diocesan quota is abnormally low for such a thriving church, and it needs to be asked whether the local family of God could be helped a little more, at the expense of some of the amount sent to missions (does Mark 7.11 apply, we wonder?). The organist appears to give his services free. Despite the big income, there is no fabric reserve account. Is this wise? Without knowing more about the parish, one does not know what is referred to as 'Fellowship help' and 'development and outreach'. It would be better to be more particular as to what this money is going to. Tax recovered is more than 33 per cent of planned giving income, so presumably most if not all planned giving is covenanted, and in addition some of the money under 'donations' is given through deposited covenants. Examinations of previous years' figures show that the church has not become complacent but that its giving increases year by year to outstrip inflation. Freely they have received and they give freely.

The budget

A copy of the model budget as given in the CBF's *Parish Account Book* is given in Appendix 6 (pp. 108–12 below). It will be seen that under 'Income' and 'Expenditure' in each case there are three columns. Last year's budget estimates are compared with the actual expenditure in the event, so that this year's estimate can be made in the light of previous experience. Overall, the budget in the previous year hoped for a surplus of £20, but ended with a surplus of £28.37. Next year the parish hopes to do a little better and finish with £135 in hand.

It will be seen from this model that the treasurer has prepared a realistic budget for a year knowing the pattern of expenditure in the previous year. Ideally he will need to have the total year's figures in front of him (unaudited) to prepare the budget; but if he prepares it a month or so before the year's end, he can always do a bit of intelligent estimating of the annual totals on the basis of ten or eleven months' figures and his knowledge from previous years of the annual pattern of receipts and payments (do annual donations all arrive in December with Christmas greetings? Is there a fuel bill to be paid that month?). The advantage of having complete and relevant information is obvious, but many treasurers feel that this leaves the adoption of the budget too late on in the year, and that a budget ought to be adopted by the PCC before the first day of the year to which it relates. Each parish must make up its own mind about that.

The budget will be drafted by the treasurer and probably discussed with the incumbent and standing committee before going to the full PCC. If the receipts and payments cannot balance without budgeting for a deficit, this must be resolved. Providing there are reserves which can be called upon, a small deficit in one year is tolerable; but unless there are exceptional reasons, to *budget* for a deficit is a very unwise thing to do. It means that the church plans to spend money it does not expect to receive. In that case, expenditure must be contained until such time as income improves, and the budget will reflect this. A budget should be monitored over the course of the year and if the position improves, a supplementary budget can be considered.

When the PCC has agreed on the budget for the year, it should be publicized so that the parishioners can know the details of how the PCC intends to spend the money it expects to receive in the year ahead.

The 'model' budget will not be adequate for every parish, because each parish has its own pattern and headings of expenditure. In particular, there are some notable omissions from the 'model'. Lay training is important; so is development work for projects within the parish. There ought to be a fabric or reserve fund, to go towards the cost of the quinquennial survey fee and work necessary as a result of this, and to form a basis from which the parish can begin to build if there need to be special efforts in order to fund emergency or quinquennial repairs.

The published headings are broad descriptions; the treasurer himself may wish to break some of them down into sub-headings for greater accuracy and control of expenditure. Such a procedure will also help to pinpoint where there have been savings or over-expenditure by the end of the year. Thus, for example, 'Working Expenses' could be broken down into 'telephone, postages, stationery, car mileage and depreciation, secretarial assistance, office equipment, maintenance of robes, hospitality, provision of locum tenens'; the item for the lay staff would be subdivided into verger, clerk, sexton, organist and choir, and so on. One way in which this might be done is shown in Appendix 7 (pp. 113–15 below).

The end of the matter

The parish treasurer is a vital person to the health of every parish, and the debt which the Church of England owes to the devoted

Christian service of its many thousands of parish treasurers is known to God alone. The treasurer is a self-effacing character. He knows that finance is a good servant, but a bad master. When a parish is so worried about money that it becomes a constant niggle at every PCC meeting, it has lost its sense of mission and direction. The good treasurer hopes that his work will go unnoticed, so that the parish can carry out its work largely unaware of the financial constraints. Parish finance is only noticed when it is going badly; like a thumb, we only remember we have one when it is sore. But we need our thumbs and we would not get very far without them. If the treasurer can take from the incumbent and the PCC the debilitating strain on their spiritual energies which is created by financial worry, he can release them for the work of the Gospel through the life of the fellowship. That is the justification for his work and the satisfaction of it.

Appendix 1
Percentage Giving Chart

To work out one's percentage giving at various levels of weekly income, lay a ruler or a straight piece of paper across the page for an immediate answer.

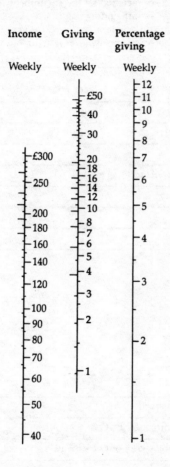

Income	Giving	Percentage giving
Weekly	Weekly	Weekly

Note:
Draw a straight line from your income figure in the first column, through the figure representing your giving in the second column, to find your percentage giving in the third column.

Appendix 2
Working Expenses Claim Form

PARISH OF

Details of parish expenses incurred by the Incumbent (or other full-time staff: see note 5) for the month ending _____ 19 _____

Please read the notes below before completing the form

	£	
Use of car: _____ miles @ _____ p per mile (See note 3)		
Public transport		
Telephone		
Postage and stationery		
Office equipment (details to be given below)		
Robes		
Hospitality		
Secretarial assistance		
Miscellaneous *Details to be given*		
Total expenditure incurred		
Reimbursed or paid direct by PCC		
Amount to be borne by clergy out of stipend		

Signed   Date

(Incumbent or other member of staff)

Notes

1 Only expenses necessarily incurred in connection with parochial duties should be claimed. Any expenses incurred in connection with other duties such as chaplaincies should not be included. The cost of heating, lighting and cleaning the parsonage and of garden upkeep should not be included.
  In any case of doubt, the Diocesan Office should be consulted.
2 Clergy and the Parochial Church Council concerned may wish to discuss the setting of agreed limits to claims under any of the heads shown.
3 The mileage rate should be that recommended by the diocese, which is notified annually to clergy and treasurers.
4 A copy of this form should be retained by the incumbent, or member of staff, for use in connection with any claim he/she may make to the Inland Revenue for tax relief on any portion of expenses not reimbursed.
5 The phrase 'or other full-time staff' includes ministers-in-charge of benefices, team vicars, curates-in-charge of conventional districts, curates, deacons, deaconesses and full-time licensed lay workers.

A SUMMARY OF THE COMPLETED MONTHLY FORMS SHOULD BE SUBMITTED TO THE DIOCESAN OFFICE BY THE PCC SECRETARY AT THE END OF EACH YEAR.

Appendix 3
Specimen Deed of Covenant (Net)

	Notes
DEED OF COVENANT	
To: Parochial Church Council of ...	
I promise to pay you for _____ years, or until I die if earlier, such a sum as after deduction of income tax at the basic rate amounts to	1
£ _____	2
each [week] [month] [quarter] [year]	3
from [the date shown below] [_____]	4

* This deed supersedes the
undermentioned deed(s) of
covenant providing for a periodic
amount of   Date of signature

		Notes
_____	_____	5
_____	_____	
Signed and delivered		6
Date		
Full name		
Address		
Witnessed by:		
Signed		
Full name		
Address		
Countersigned on behalf of the Council		7

Explanatory Notes on the Deed of Covenant

This deed is intended to meet as many requirements of covenantors as possible in one form.

The numbers below refer to the numbers on the face of the deed.

1 Enter the period of the covenant, which must be longer than *three* years.
2 Enter the amount you will be paying to the Charity.
3 Delete as appropriate to show how often you will make the payment.
4 Delete as appropriate. If you choose to enter an actual date *it must not be earlier than the date you sign the deed.*
5 If a previous deed or deeds will be superseded, insert the amount(s) and the date(s) of such deed(s).
6 You must sign the form and enter the date you actually sign it in the presence of a witness, who should also sign where shown.
7 Deed to be countersigned on behalf of the Council if an entry has been made at 5.
   This superseding clause is only necessary when a donor wishes to increase an existing deed during its currency.

BANKER'S ORDER

To _____ Bank Ltd

_____ *(Address)*

Please pay _____ Bank

_____ *(Branch title)*

☐☐-☐☐-☐☐ *(Code number)*

for the credit of the **Parochial church council** of

_____

Account number ☐☐☐☐☐☐☐☐☐

the sum of £ _____ *(Figures)*

_____ *(Words)*

on _____ *(Date of first payment)*

and thereafter on _____ *(Date and frequency)*

until _____ *(Date of last payment)*

and debit my account.

The following existing orders are hereby cancelled.

_____

_____

Name of account to be debited _____

Account number ☐☐☐☐☐☐☐☐☐

Date _____

Signature _____

Address _____

(**Note**: the use of a Banker's Order is optional)

Appendix 4
Specimen Sheet of Deeds of Covenant Register

Deed No.	Name	Address	Amount of Deed	Date of Deed	First payment due
1	A. B. Cree	Cherry Tree, Grape Lane	£800	1.3.89	1.4.89 (annual)
2	D. E. Free	10 Charles Street	£104	24.9.89	1.12.89 (quarterly)
3	G. H. Iles	Fairways, North Road	£300	1.10.89	1.10.89 (annual) £1,200 deposited
4	J. K. Lee	1 Smith Street	£52	2.1.91	2.1.91 (weekly)
5	A. B. Cree	Cherry Tree, Grape Lane	£1,000	1.3.91	1.4.91 (half-yearly)
6	M. N. Orange	5 George Street	£50	1.3.91	5.3.91 (annual)
7	P. Q. Rust	16 Rydale Tce	£480	6.4.91	1.5.91 (monthly)

1st year	2nd year	3rd year	4th year	5th year
£800 1.4.89 £ † tax rec'd 1.7.89	£800 2.4.90 £ † tax rec'd 21.7.90	Deed of substitution – see no. 5		
£26 1.12.89 £26 3.3.90 £ † tax rec'd 21.7.90	£26 1.6.90 £26 1.9.90 £ † tax rec'd 1.8.91	Cancelled – left the area		
£300 1.10.89 £ † tax rec'd 21.7.90	£300 1.10.90 £ † tax rec'd 1.8.91			
£13 (weekly)* £ † tax rec'd 1.8.91				
£500 1.4.91** £ † tax rec'd 1.8.91	£500 1.10.91			
£50 5.3.91 £ † tax rec'd 1.8.91		Deceased July 1991		

* In this case £39 will be due in the 5th year, thus completing four full contributions of £52.

** In this case £500 will be due in the 5th year, thus completing four full contributions of £1,000.

† Enter amounts actually received.

Appendix 4 (cont.) Notes on deeds of covenant register:

Deed no. 1 started in the ordinary way as an annual deed, but after two payments, the donor signed a Deed of substitution – this fact is noted on line 1 and the new deed is entered as deed no. 5.

Deed no. 2 is for quarterly payments. In the first tax year only two contributions were received and after the receipt of the two quarterly amounts in the second year, the donor left the area and the PCC agreed to allow the deed to lapse.

Deed no. 3 is a deposited covenant. £1,200 donated but tax recoverable over four years, so the deed promises £300 p.a. for four years: no further payments required from donor.

Deed no. 4 is for £1 per week. Only 13 weekly amounts were received in the first tax year and, if it runs its full term, there will be three full years and the balance of 39 weekly contributions will be payable in the fifth year.

Deed no. 5 promises half-yearly contributions, only one half-yearly amount received before the end of the tax year; there will be three full years and the last half-yearly payment will be made in the fifth year.

Deed no. 6 was signed by a donor who died before the second payment was due. No claim can be made on his estate for the three months April/July. No further tax can be claimed. The tax received does not have to be repaid to the Inland Revenue.

Deed no. 7 is an ordinary deed signed in the current tax year, and twelve monthly contributions not yet received.

Appendix 5
Loan or Deposited Covenant letter

Dear

I enclose a deed of covenant and a cheque for £ _____, being a deposit free
of interest which, subject as provided below, is repayable to me on
demand. You are hereby authorized and requested to hold the deposit on
my behalf, so that each year the sum of £ _____ may be deducted and so
constitute the annual payments due under my Deed dated _____.

* I hereby waive repayment of such part of the deposit as may remain at
the date of my death to the intent that such instalments shall remain the
property of your PCC.

_____

Signature of donor

* This paragraph is optional, but if it is included, as it would affect the estate of a
deceased person, two independent witnesses must countersign the letter. If the
donor dies after making the first payment, or after the due date in a subsequent tax
year, the R 185(AP) may be signed by the executor(s).

Appendix 6
Model Budget

_____ Parochial Church Council

BUDGET FOR THE YEAR ENDING 31 DECEMBER 1987

	Budget 1987 £	Agreed budget 1986 £	Expected result from 1986 £
The ministry			
Incumbent:			
Stipend, Easter offering, allowances	360	320	320
Housing	280	250	260
Working expenses	1,160	1,140	1,120
The church and services			
Heating, lighting, cleaning	1,100	1,000	960
Insurance	560	520	536
Minor repairs	250	250	204
Upkeep of services: altar, books, robes, music	400	230	231
Churchyard	250	300	294
Other ordinary expenditure			
Lay staff salaries, wages, honoraria	400	580	600
Church hall	500	600	596
Sunday school	120	120	110
Christian stewardship	60	50	52
Magazines, bookstall	180	150	180
Administration, printing, stationery, postage, sundries	250	220	220
The diocese			
Quota – general	1,215	1,080	1,077
stipends	3,300	3,080	3,082
parsonages	240	190	192
Payments to charities			
Church overseas:			
missionary societies	500	400	458
relief and development agencies	200	150	150
Home missions, other Church societies	100	100	126
Other charities	100	80	100
Extraordinary payments			
Repairs to church tower		1,000	1,000
Loans	–	–	–
Transfers (Budget of Opportunity: parish project)	2,000	–	–
Surplus of income over expenditure for the year	135	20	8
	13,660	11,830	11,876

	Budget 1987	Agreed budget 1986	Expected result from 1986
	£	£	£
Voluntary receipts			
Planned giving:			
Covenants including Income Tax recoverable	5,700	5,200	5,400
Uncovenanted	570	600	580
Collection boxes:			
General purposes	1,330	1,390	1,330
Missions, charities	800	750	780
Easter, Whitsun offerings	230	230	221
Gift days, fetes, bazaars, other fund-raising events	1,200	1,200	1,091
Magazines, bookstall	170	150	163
Sundry donations	120	120	100
Other ordinary receipts			
Fees	170	180	170
Dividends and interest	170	170	167
Church hall	800	700	695
Trusts	–	60	59
Grants	400	380	380
Extraordinary receipts			
Donations, appeals	2,000	450	490
Non-recurring grants	–	250	250
Loans	–	–	–
Transfers	–	–	–
	13,660	11,830	11,876

Similar budgets can be compiled for other funds

Appendix 6

INCOME AND EXPENDITURE ACCOUNT FOR THE YEAR ENDED 31 DECEMBER 1986

GENERAL ACCOUNT

Expenditure

1985
£

		£	£	£
	The ministry			
	Incumbent:			
290	Stipend, Easter offering, allowances	320.00		
170	Housing	260.00		
1,063	Working expenses	1,122.10	1,702.10	
	The church and services			
940	Heating, lighting, cleaning	976.32		
509	Insurance	536.12		
377	Minor repairs	204.00		
219	Upkeep of services:			
	altar, books, robes, music	230.75		
209	Churchyard	294.41		
534	Lay staff salaries, wages, honoraria	584.00	2,825.60	
	Other ordinary expenditure			
500	Church hall	596.50		
–	PCC property	–		
137	Sunday school	101.00		
103	Christian stewardship	52.65		
143	Magazines, bookstall	171.70		
213	Administration, printing, stationery,			
	postage, sundries	212.04	1,133.89	
	The diocese			
995	General	1,077.00		
2,770	Stipends	3,082.00		
188	Parsonages	192.00	4,351.00	
	Payments to charities			
	Church Overseas			
379	missionary societies	503.36		
130	relief and development agencies	161.00		
107	Home missions, other Church societies	125.80		
80	Other charities	107.00	897.16	10,909.75
	Extraordinary expenditure			
1,500	Repairs to church tower			980.00
–	Excess of income over expenditure			28.37
11,556				11,918.12

Income
1985
£

		£	£	£
	Voluntary income			
	Planned giving:			
3,207	Net covenants	3,605.00		
1,642	Income tax received on covenants	1,843.42		
593	Uncovenanted	584.50	6,032.92	
	Collection boxes:			
1,382	General purposes	1,313.79		
620	Missions, charities	791.40		
210	Easter, Whitsun offerings	221.10		
1,331	Gift days, fetes, bazaars, other fund-raising events	1,090.88		
148	Magazines, bookstall	163.02		
80	Sundry donations	97.65	3,677.84	
	Other ordinary income			
172	Fees	166.00		
170	Dividends and interest	167.35		
680	Church hall	694.90		
–	PCC property	–		
59	Trusts	59.00		
350	Grants	380.00	1,467.25	11,178.01
	Extraordinary income			
332	Donations, appeals, etc.	490.11		
–	Non-recurring grants	250.00		
500	Legacies	–		
50	Insurance claims	–		
				740.11
30	Excess of expenditure over income			–
11,556				11,918.12

Similar accounts can be compiled for other funds

Appendix 6

_____ Parochial Church Council

BALANCE SHEET AS AT 31 DECEMBER 1986

	£	£	£
Permanent assets			
Property at cost (if applicable)			–
Investments			
950 shares in the CBF Investment Fund (at cost)			2,850.00
(Market value at 31.12.86: £3,979.55)			
Current assets			
Cash on deposit with the CBF Deposit Fund		500.00	
Cash at bank		815.45	
Cash in hand		170.00	
		————	
		1,485.45	
Amounts due to the PCC		230.00	
Amounts paid by the PCC in advance		–	
		————	
		1,715.45	
less			
Current liabilities			
Bank overdraft (if applicable)	–		
Loans to the PCC	–		
Amounts owed by the PCC	91.00		
Amounts received by the PCC in advance	100.00		
	————		
		191.00	
		————	
			1,524.45
			————
			4,374.45
			————
Represented by:			
Accumulated fund			
Balance at 1.1.86			4,346.08
Add excess of income over expenditure			28.37
			————
			4,374.45
			————

Appendix 7
Suggested budget sub-divisions

This 'extended budget' may be of help in the preparation of the main budget items and may help to highlight any particular headings where big increases may be necessary as compared with the previous year. This is for guidance only and should be adapted to meet local circumstances.

Income budget
Voluntary receipts:
   Planned or pledged giving
   Covenants including income tax recoverable
   Uncovenanted
Collections – including collection boxes
   Collections (other than pledged and covenanted giving) at all services to be used for ordinary purposes
   Earmarked collections:
      Missions and charities
      Easter and Whitsun offerings – if earmarked
Gift days, fetes, bazaars and other fund-raising events for ordinary purposes
Magazines/bookstall
Sundry donations
Other ordinary receipts:
   Fees (weddings, funerals etc.)
   Dividends and interest including any reclaimed tax
   Church hall lettings etc.
   Rent from land or other buildings owned by PCC
   Trusts
   Grants
Extraordinary receipts:
   Donations, appeals
   Non-recurring grants
   Loans
   Transfers

Expenditure budget
Incumbent – stipend, parsonage house and working expenses:
   Stipend (direct or through diocese)
   Parsonage house
     – repair assessment (this item could be entered under 'Diocese')
     – water rates
     – interior redecoration
     – ......
   Working expenses
     – telephone
     – postages

- stationery
- car/public transport
- secretarial assistance
- office equipment
- maintenance of robes
- hospitality
- provision of locum tenens

Assistant staff (mainly as for incumbent)

Visiting clergy and speakers

Church – running expenses
  heating
  lighting
  cleaning
    – wages and National Insurance
    – materials
  water rate
  insurance premium

Church maintenance
  minor repairs including routine maintenance
  organ/piano tuning
  care of church grounds

Upkeep of services:
  altar requisites
  repair and replacement of service books, music, leaflets, choir robes

Upkeep of churchyard:
  routine maintenance including wages and contracts
  repair of mower and other equipment
  grass cutting

Salaries/wages/honoraria (and National Insurance where applicable)
  verger
  clerk
  sexton
  organist
  choir

Hall:
  water rate
  routine maintenance and repair
  insurance premium
  heating
  lighting
  cleaning equipment

Other PCC property
  various items as for hall

Education
  Church day school
  Sunday school
  lay training
  other educational expenses

Other ordinary parish expenditure:
   Administration:
      – printing
      – stationery
      – postages
      – audit and other fees
      – bank charges and loan interest
        . . . . . .
        . . . . . .
   Christian stewardship annual expenses
   donations or gifts to sick and poor of parish (or incumbent's
      discretionary fund)
   expenditure on parish magazine and bookstall
   outings, treats etc.
Diocese and deanery:
   quota or share
   contribution to deanery expenses/quota/share
   other payments to diocese or deanery
Missionary and charitable giving:
   recognized missionary societies and other overseas missions
   home missions and other church societies and organizations
   secular charities
Capital development (not classed as routine)
   Church:
      major repairs (structure)
      major repairs/replacements (installations)
      interior and exterior re-decoration
   Hall: as above
   New building or major works:
      parsonage house
      housing for curate/lay worker/caretaker etc.
      church
      hall
   Non-recurring costs of stewardship campaign
   Repayment of loans (excluding interest)
   Transfers to reserves
      e.g. for church/hall/housing
         for purchase of investments
Other development work as agreed by PCC for the year concerned

Appendix 8
Bank Reconciliation

A specimen bank reconciliation is given below:

	£
Balance as per bank statement on 31 May	210.67
Add details of amounts entered in cash book on or before 31 May but not yet paid into bank	50.48
	261.15
Less details of cheques dated and entered in cash book on or before 31 May and not yet included in bank statement	31.79
Balance in cash book at 31 May	229.36

Cash book:

	£
Receipts to 31 May	6,543.21
Payments	6,313.85
	229.36

As advised on p. 83, this reconciliation process should be carried out frequently (monthly?) and the bank should be asked to provide statements at appropriate intervals to enable this to be done. At the end of the financial year it is useful to write out the reconciliation in full in the cash book, to help both the treasurer and the auditor.

Appendix 9
Booklist

The Canons of the Church of England, being Canons Ecclesiastical promulged by the Convocations of Canterbury and York in 1964 and 1969 and by the General Synod of the Church of England from 1970 (Church House Publishing, 4th edition 1986; loose leaf. Supplements are issued from time to time to bring the publication up to date)

The Church Log Book (CHP, loose-leaf edition 1980)

Church Representation Rules, being Schedule 3 of the Synodical Government Measure 1969 as subsequently amended (CHP, 1990)

The Churchyards Handbook, Peter Burman and Henry Stapleton (CHP, 3rd edition 1988)

County and Voluntary Schools, Kenneth Brooksbank and David Nice (Longman Group UK Ltd in association with the Society of Education Officers, 7th edition, 1989)

A Handbook for Churchwardens and Parochial Church Councillors, Kenneth M. Macmorran, E. Garth Moore and Timothy Briden (Mowbray, 1989 edition)

Organists' Guide to Employment (Incorporated Society of Musicians, 1990)

Parish Account Book (CHP, 1987)

Terrier and Inventory, as authorized by the General Synod of the Church of England 1972 (CHP, 1982)

Appendix 10
Measures referred to (all HMSO publications)

Care of Churches and Ecclesiastical Jurisdiction Measure 1991
Church Funds Investment Measure 1958
Church of England (Legal Aid and Miscellaneous Provisions) Measure 1988
Church of England (Pensions) Measures 1961–1988
Ecclesiastical Fees Measure 1962
Ecclesiastical Officers (Age Limit) Measure 1975
Endowments and Glebe Measure 1976
Faculty Jurisdiction Measure 1964
Incumbents and Churchwardens (Trusts) Measure 1964
Inspection of Churches Measure 1955
Parochial Church Councils (Powers) Measure 1956
Pastoral Measure 1983
Repair of Benefice Buildings Measure 1972
Sharing of Church Buildings Act 1969 (Act of Parliament – not a Measure of the General Synod)
Synodical Government Measure 1969

Appendix 11
Addresses

Central Board of Finance of the Church of England, Church House, Great Smith Street, Westminster, London SW1P 3NZ

Central Board of Finance Investment Office, St Alphage House, 2 Fore Street, London EC2Y 5AQ

Charities Aid Foundation, 48 Pembury Road, Tonbridge, Kent TN9 2JD

Charity Commissioners, Graeme House, Derby Square, Liverpool L2 7SB and St Alban's House, 57/60 Haymarket, London SW1Y 4QX

Church Commissioners, 1 Millbank, London SW1P 3JZ

Church Finance Supplies Ltd, Radley Road Industrial Estate, Radley Road, Abingdon-on-Thames OX14 3SE

Church House Bookshop, 31 Great Smith Street, London SW1P 3BN

Church of England Pensions Board, 7 Little College Street, London SW1P 3SF

Ecclesiastical Insurance Group plc, Beaufort House, Brunswick Road, Gloucester GL1 1JZ

General Synod Board of Education and the National Society, Church House, Great Smith Street, Westminster, London SW1P 3NZ

Incorporated Society of Musicians, 10 Stratford Place, London W1N 9AE

Inland Revenue Claims Branch (Charity Division), St John's House, Merton Road, Stanley Precinct, Bootle, Merseyside L69 4EJ

Official Custodian for Charities, St Alban's House, 57/60 Haymarket, London SW1Y 4QZ

Royal College of Organists, Kensington Gore, London SW7 2QS

Royal School of Church Music, Addington Palace, Croydon, Surrey CR9 5AD

Index